You Reject Them, You Reject Me

The Prison Letters of Joan Andrews

YOU REJECT THEM, YOU REJECT ME

The Prison Letters of Joan Andrews

Richard Cowden Guido, Ed.

TRINITY COMMUNICATIONS
MANASSAS, VIRGINIA

ISBN   0-937495-25-5, cloth
          0-937495-26-3, paper

First printing May 1988
Second printing September 1988
Changes: Emendations of several letters
               Insertion of letter of Mother Teresa, p. 22
               New concluding remarks, pp. 222-223

To those for whom Joan Andrews stands in witness.

"How often an imprisonment has radically changed the direction of national or global affairs. Take away the names of all the noble prisoners from history, and there will not be enough spiritual energy to run the world."

Jaime Cardinal Sin
Archbishop of Manila

Acknowledgements

To Judie Brown for her gracious leave, and her support for Joan and Joan's cause. To Jeff Mirus for his insight and confidence. To all of the Andrews family: with a special thanks to Susan and Miriam, the one who got it all started; and to Elizabeth Andrews, for her determination to protect her daughter's witness, and not least for the wonderful batch of letters from the early years. And to Joan herself, for letting me peer into the more private recesses of her life, and for our happy phone conversations and editing together.

To T. H. and Joe Wall and Peter Lennox and Juli Loesch and Earl Essex and Diane Bodner and all the people who kindly sent me Joan's correspondence. To all those I am neglecting here, but who have prayed and worked for Joan, and who have worked for justice. As ever to the Italian beauty who married me, and who provides my happiest inspirations. And finally to Brent Bozell, Michael Schwartz and Triumph magazine for organizing the first rescue I know of, in 1970 in Washington D.C., three years before *Roe v. Wade*.

Caveats

Apart from the ellipses and not always starting Joan's letters at the beginning, there has only been slight editing of the passages here published. The most extensive was in Joan's letter to Joe Scheidler, which in addition to polishing some expression, adds some three sentences in order to elaborate her theory and practice of non-cooperation.

You Reject Them, You Reject Me

Introduction

I first talked about Joan Andrews with Nat Hentoff in October 1987. Hentoff, a self-described unreconstructed atheist Jew, is also a rare gem of New Yorker and American: he is an honest liberal. Very liberal, too; he is an idealist on free speech, indeed made his reputation by his defense of First Amendment absolutism. As a jazz critic, a 30-year veteran of the *Village Voice*, a columnist for the Washington *Post* and much more, Hentoff's reasoning is not always his principal distinction, though he reasons better than most. His principle distinction is his hunger for justice.

It leads him up some strange trails. Thus, though Hentoff has been a confidante of William Brennan, William Douglas and other Supreme Court Justices, he repudiates the reasoning of *Roe v. Wade*, the 1973 Supreme Court decision legalizing abortion-on-demand in the United States. In fact, it was clear throughout the 1970's Hentoff was uncomfortable with abortion, and in 1975 his wife Margot wrote a blistering defense of the unborn in the *Voice*. It was not until 1983, however, that Hentoff explicitly condemned legal abortion; he did so after preparing an 18-part investigative series on the widespread practice and theoretical defense of infanticide, the killing of children born alive, in the United States.

Even then, though calling for the overthrow of *Roe*, he hesi-
tated about imposing legal sanctions against abortionists. In
an August 1987 phone conversation, however, he argued
that the mothers of the aborted child should be legally regarded as victims of assault, able, among other things to sue
any abortionist's assets. Society itself, he then acknowledged,
is obliged to put the abortionist in jail.

Though I have never asked her, I suspect Joan Andrews
holds a similar view. Believe it or not, the depth of her
Catholic faith would I know inspire her to anxiety for the
abortionist as well; which might be why, given the threat of
their trade to their souls, jailing them would be a charitable
act. Reading her letters about what jail is like, I'm not so
sure on that point, though it would certainly be charitable to
their victims; for whom, as presumably the reader knows,
Joan Andrews has an especial regard.

But not only Joan. The explosive political undercurrent
of the abortion wars took some hard turns in 1987. The
bombings of abortion centers decreased significantly, though
there were some significant exceptions. What increased, was
the number of pro-life counseling centers across the country;
the constant demonstrations outside the abortion centers;
and the number and success of tactical sit-ins, for one of
which Joan Andrews was sentenced to five years in prison in
September of 1986.

On the pro-abortion side, state courts in 1987 ruled for
the first time that patients could be starved to death, even
without their permission, if their family decides that's probably what the patient would want—and this, even if the family
stands economically to benefit. Infanticide, though theoretically restrained by laws passed not a little due to Hentoff's
18-part series, in fact made eerie advances: for the first time,
hospitals agreed to keep children scheduled for abortion
alive until after a forced premature birth, so that their body
parts could be cut out (while they are still alive) in order to

assist the health of others. As for abortion itself, it went on, state financed and unabated, four to five thousand times a day in the United States. The fate of those thousands was revealed in a series of exposés that appeared throughout the year in different American cities.

"When we pulled our cars slowly into the dark alley behind the Michigan Avenue Medical Center," wrote Monica Miglorino in the July 1987 *Fidelity*, "rats scurried before our headlights, frightened by the noise of our intrusion. . . . We had stopped in front of a loading dock upon which stood three garbage dumpsters and a trash barrel. . . .

"We all climbed onto the loading dock," Ms. Milgorino continues, "opened the dumpsters, and began to look through the trash. I opened a red dumpster and yanked out one or two bags of garbage from the Michigan Medical Center [in downtown Chicago] . . . As we pulled out of the alley, the rats once again darted in front of our headlights . . .

"We drove to Joe Scheidler's garage in order to examine the contents of the box. The box was sealed with silver duct tape which we carefully peeled off. Inside were 43 small, plastic 'specimen' bags. Each bag contained the mutilated body of an aborted baby, complete with placenta and uterine tissue. Several of the bags were marked with a tag upon which was scribbled the name of the aborted baby's mother, her age, the date of the abortion, and a number . . . though many of the children were quite small, one could plainly see through the plastic their little arms, legs, hands, feet, rib cages, spinal columns, eyes (often out of their sockets), and sometimes even heads and faces."

"The abortionists throw all that in the garbage," noted *National Review* senior editor Joseph Sobran about similar discoveries in the nation's capital. The babies themselves, he wrote, in a nationally syndicated column, "are colorless, drained of blood, smelling of formaldehyde. They were aborted at about 10 to 20 weeks after their conception. Some are 2 inches long, some eight inches, and might have been longer if they had heads. The abortionist usually has to crush the head to pull the body through the mother's undilated cervix. One of the smaller ones still has part of her face. Her tongue, a small white tab, is hanging out, and her eyes bulge."

About a boy, Sobran writes, "the lower half of his body is pretty much intact. From the waist up there is only the naked spinal cord, plus the right shoulder, arm and hand. His legs are spread apart, with the knees bent and pointing away from each other . . . you notice his genitals, his calf muscles and his feet. His toes are curled tensely upward, as if he died in the middle of a spasm . . . you could see, and smell, the fresh blood. These children had been killed that day."

"Most of the bodies of children killed in Washington," noted the pacifist John Cavanaugh-O'Keefe in his newsletter, "are now in the Lorton landfill, food for vermin."

*   *   *

In March 1986 Joan Andrews entered a Pensacola, Florida abortion center, tried unsuccessfully to pull the plug from a suction machine, and offered passive resistance to her arrest for seeking to block the commerce described above. Instead of trespassing, Andrews was charged with burglary, malicious mischief, resisting arrest and assault—which latter charge in Florida carries a life sentence. When she refused not to engage even in legal actions against abortion ("I couldn't promise not to save a child's life," she told the Judge, "to me, that's scandalous."), bail was denied. For four months she remained in prison under the prospect of a life sentence until the assault charges were dropped because they were false.

After conviction in a non-jury trial by Judge William Anderson in July, Andrews announced that "the only way I can protest for unborn children now is by non-cooperation in jail"—whereupon she sat in the middle of the courtroom and had to be carried back to Escambia County Jail. Because of her "noncooperation" policy (as she calls it), Andrews was put in solitary confinement; and in an interpretation of the First Amendment Nat Hentoff (among others) finds curious, Andrews was denied the right to attend Mass as part of the punishment.

So it continued until her sentencing on 24 September. Florida guidelines recommend a year to thirty months maximum for convicted burglars. Judge Anderson, however, was not pleased that Andrews's political position of non-cooperation hadn't even been broken by—illegally, according to Hentoff—denying her right to a Catholic Mass. He warned her in open court that prison officials have "their ways" of ensuring cooperation; and then he sentenced her to five years in prison. Later that day he gave four-year sentences to two men convicted of accessory to murder.

Judge Anderson's confidence, however, was ill-founded. Prison officials and State authority did indeed have "ways" to ensure cooperation; but none of them moved Andrews. She would not sign papers or participate in prison activities. When solitary confinement and denying her Mass didn't break her, she was transferred first to medium security at Lowell, then to Broward Correctional Institute in Miami, the maximum security prison for Florida's most dangerous female inmates. She was then placed among Broward's most dangerous, those who were in disciplinary confinement because they had committed further crimes while in prison. One of her letters describes the initiation.

"Broward," she writes, "certainly looks more like one's idea of a 'real prison' than Lowell did . . . you should see the landscape in which Broward is set. It's all surrounded by desolate brush and land and the prison is isolated by itself in the barren wasteland. The buildings are two and three-storey buildings grouped together. One interesting point is that the buildings are all painted white with blue (Blessed Mother blue) markings. However, inside the close custody building, everything looks most stark and brutal. Death Row and the Reception and Orientation (R&O) quarters occupy one wing, and then behind two locked doors is the confinement lock-up of Disciplinary Confinement and Administrative Confinement (DC & AC) inmates.

"When I informed the R&O sergeant that I could not cooperate, things got a little ruffled for awhile. A crew of staff came in. Finally the Lieutenant in charge gave me a tour of the confinement wing to scare me into changing my mind. He kept saying, 'You'll be behind these locks for five years,' and 'This is a maximum security prison, not a jail. You'll never see anything like this!' and, 'I have my roughest inmates in here and this prison only takes close custody inmates, and do you think I'm going to waste one of my limited confinement cells on you?' I told him he had to handle the situation the way he saw best, but that I had to do also what I had to do. I told him I could not cooperate, that if he wanted me in R&O or anywhere, he'd have to carry me. . . .

"Finally they had a big conference, while I waited out near the death row cells. Then the Lieutenant and a Sergeant took me to the medical building to be checked out by a psychiatrist to see if I was crazy . . . he turned to the two officers and answered their questions about my sanity by saying: 'No, she's not crazy nor mentally ill. She simply has very strongly held beliefs. She's perfectly normal.' And that was that."

It was not her only description of prison life, however. About Lowell, she wrote the following a month previous to the letter above.

"I am doing well. My cell is a regular single cell, breccia block and concrete and steel. My area is called West Confinement, and it houses twenty-five solitary confinement cells for disciplinary problems (like me!). We are allowed two free letters a week to send out. While in disciplinary lock-up, we cannot receive commissary (thus I can't buy stamps), nor have visitors, nor have any books except religious ones (that's fine!). We do get out in a small exercise yard, where we stand around, or, better yet, walk through the yard while praying the rosary. It's just for Disciplinary Prisoners, but since we must undergo a strip search after every yard-out, I don't plan to go often. It's one hour each day, except Saturday and Sunday. At any rate, I get enough exercise walking in my cell during the rosaries and mercy of God devotionals.

"Across the corridor from my cell is a window which is partially open, so it's really great to get the fresh air after none at Escambia. The view is of grass and trees and part of the other buildings of the compound, and the usual: barbed wire fences, *et al.* Still, a scenic view compared to Escambia County Jail. There are no TV's here, a real blessing, but the inmates 'go off' often, and there is often screaming and crying, cursing and violent tantrums. It's so sad. The place exaggerates the fears and hostility and loneliness of prison because these feelings become concentrated during the long periods of solitary confinement unless you rely on God.

"The first night I was here, October 1st, one lady made strange animal noises all night—they were different animal cries of pain, and so were beyond the animal and were grippingly scary, as though she had broken mentally. After hours of wailing, very loudly, then very low, a decent officer went in and, I think, must have held her, because the cries slowed down and became much subdued. I think they sent her to Chattahoochie, the state mental hospital, a dreadful place with the most horrific reputation. Pray for her. I hope she is all right."

At Escambia, where Andrews lived from April to October, "it was rumored that I had been strip searched in the most objectionable way—with cavity searches. The latter is incorrect. I was strip searched, but there were no cavity searches. The reason I refused further visits was that the searches were done at night in a large, brightly-lit holding tank facing large out-door windows [in full view of correctional] officers, male and female. . . . Two inmates would be stripped together at a time, thus affording no privacy on any score. I refused to cooperate in the way it was being done, and I was subsequently forcibly stripped. I went limp and was handcuffed, dragged across the cell to the bars, and stripped and searched by two female officers."

The reader should recall that Miss Andrews need not have undergone any of this, could have stopped it at any time, simply by abandoning her position of noncooperation. Indeed, had she accepted a plea bargain, or conditional probation, or made virtually any gesture at all acknowledging the State's right to defend the abortion industry, she would have been freed from jail altogether. This is, for eminently comprehensible reasons, in fact the route chosen by the two other women and one man who were arrested with Andrews for the March 1986 sit-in (one of whom, 20-year-old Karissa Epperly, was nursing her two-month old child at the time of the arrest). Epperly was released in July, the other two in August 1986; that is, just at the time Andrews began what is now her eighteen-month sojourn—the entire time illegally denied her First Amendment right to a Catholic Mass—in solitary confinement among the most dangerous female prisoners in Florida.

Leaving aside the breakdown Andrews' witness has provoked in the American legal system, the human question necessarily arises—why doesn't she just give in? It is one thing to talk about conscience, but what prevents her from making some simple compromises of the kind for which no one would blame her, and which would have saved her all the suffering this collection of letters will reveal? The answer to that question, and the formidable nature of the threat she poses to the abortion culture, is arguably provided in a letter she wrote on 15 July 1986, a week before Judge Anderson convicted her of burglary.

"The closer we are to the preborn children," she wrote at that time, "the more faithful we are, then the more identically aligned we become with them. This is our aim, and goal, to wipe out the line of distinction between the preborn and their born friends, becoming ourselves discriminated against. Good! This is necessary. Why should we be treated any differently?

"The rougher it gets for us," she continued, "the more we can rejoice that we are succeeding; no longer are we being treated so much as the privileged born, but as the discriminated against preborn. We must become aligned with them completely and totally or else the double standard separating the preborn from the rest of humanity will never be eliminated. I don't want to be treated any differently than my brother, my sister. You reject them, you reject me.

"We do not expect justice in the courts. Furthermore we do not seek it for ourselves when it is being denied our beloved preborn brothers and sisters. Thus I plead a case for complete and total vulnerability in court by refusing self defense and all legal argumentation for *self* protection. We should in truth tell the court that we, as defenders and friends of the preborn, expect no justice and no compassion, as the true defendants, the preborn children, received none and were killed without due process on the day of the rescue attempt. We only stand here in their stead, being substitute defendants by a compelling and painful logic. They died for the crimes of being preborn and unwanted. We expect no justice from a judicial system which decrees such savagery and a government which allows it. If it is a crime punishable by death to be unwanted, maybe it should be a crime, punishable by death, to love the unwanted and to act to protect them."

*   *   *

There has been something missing from the pro-life movement, from the beginning. The enormity of what abortion is has always demanded something more than magazine articles and politicians, though no one denies the vital necessity of those things as well. But for all the unsung, amazing willingness to sacrifice on the part of so many pro-lifers across the country, and world, there has been missing from that sacrifice an element Joan Andrews has now introduced.

This book is a collection mostly of clips from Joan's prison letters, but some others as well, along with a few articles and anecdotes relating to her story. They tell it vividly, and I believe those who read them will come away with the same eerie impression that struck me as I read them.

It is this: The abortion culture cannot long endure the witness of a Joan Andrews. Either it will kill her, or she, by the grace of God, will destroy it. If you think I exaggerate, read on. The end of the abortion culture may be at hand.

Richard Cowden Guido

The Letters

You express a great deal of anxiety over our willingness to break laws. This is certainly a legitimate concern . . . One may well ask: 'How can you advocate breaking some laws and obeying others?' The answer lies in the fact that there are two types of laws: just and unjust. I would be the first to advocate obeying just laws. One has not only a legal but a moral responsibility to obey just laws. Conversely, one has a moral responsibility to disobey unjust laws. I would agree with St. Augustine that 'an unjust law is no law at all.'

Now, what is the difference between the two? How does one determine whether a law is just or unjust? A just law is a man-made code that squares with the moral law or the law of God. An unjust law is a code that is out of harmony with the moral law. To put it in the terms of St. Thomas Aquinas: an unjust law is a human law that is not rooted in eternal law and natural law.

Dr. Martin Luther King, Jr.
Nobel Peace Laureate
Letter from a Birmingham Jail

1

Story in The Marshall Gazette, Lewisburg, Tennessee:
4 April 1978

It's not if you win the race, it's how you ride. That could
have been the words of praise for Miriam Andrews when she
entered the Point-to-Point race at Maple Grove Farm in
Nashville Saturday, March 25. Miriam and her sister Joan
are training thoroughbred horses at the farm of their parents
Mr. and Mrs. W. L. Andrews here and plan an exciting summer.

Miriam was the rider of Seuter Le Canon, a horse with
much potential in the racing circles, and was so impressive
she was offered a job by Paul Sloan, who won the event, after the race. . . . For a time Seuter and Miriam were running
first and second but because the horse wasn't in shape at this
time, they were not in the winning circle.

They plan to steeple-chase until this summer and then
take the horse to enter it in the events at Churchill Downs
and Ellis Park in Kentucky. In addition to Seuter, the Andrews sisters are training two other thoroughbred horses at
this time. Joan acts as trainer of the horses and Miriam will

ride in all events. Miriam just graduated from high school and is taking courses at Columbia State but her first love is horses.

Letter from Mrs. Elizabeth Andrews: January 1988

Joan was born Sunday, March 7, 1948 at 4:25 a.m. at Old St. Thomas Hospital, across from the Cathedral of the Incarnation in Nashville, Tennessee. She was baptized the following Sunday, March 14, at Christ the King Church, with her grandparents, Edward & Jessica Early, chosen to be her godparents. Joan was the third child. Her brother Bill was two years older and her brother John one year older. Her sister Susan was born one year following Joan's birth.

Joan's father, William L. Andrews, was working at Bell Telephone Company in Nashville and had started working on rate cases in the legal department. Eventually he decided to leave Bell, and we moved to the family farm in Lewisburg, Tennessee in 1951, that his father had bought just before he died in 1924, when William was eight. It seemed a daring adventure, for we had never lived on a farm, but it turned out to be the most beautiful experience in the family's life.

Each of the children made their first Holy Communion in second grade. . . . [T]heir father decided to teach school in Santa Fe, Tennessee. . . . [T]o the great joy of all the family, son David was born in 1957, followed by the joy of Miriam being born in 1959. . . . There was always something exciting on the farm for the children: the shearing of sheep, the plowing, the disking, the seeding of a pasture, the raking, the bailing of hay.

From the very earliest age, the boys in their room, the girls in theirs, and I in the rocker between, said a very fervent rosary each night. All of us saying this rosary together each night was a great joy. We had Mass at our mission church each Sunday in Lewisburg.

Joan was 12 years old when on a family picnic on Duck

river near the farm. A cousin went further downstream (unbeknownst to the family), where the water was deep and treacherous. On this summer day, we all heard the chilling shrieks and then saw the bobbing, disappearing head of the children's cousin. Joan rushed to that point and dove into the gushing water, reached her cousin, and bore her up, while Joan herself was under water. Bill and John pushed a log up which buoyed her cousin and Joan up until they reached shore. Joan fell face down on the shore. She got up and said, "I was underwater and held her feet on my shoulders. I knew I was going to die, but you have to do something, you have to try."

In 1966, Joan was graduated from St. Bernard Academy and entered Saint Louis University as a freshman that fall. . . . During the period of the late 60's and early 70's, Joan wrote many manuscripts. Many of her writings centered around Nazi Germany and the holocaust of the Jews under Hitler. Joan's true great heroes of that period were Raoul Wallenburg, who saved so many Jews during the Nazi atrocities, and Monsignor Hugh O'Flaherty, who also fought for the Jews in the shadow of the Vatican during the Nazi occupation of Rome.

Her reading tastes ran especially to Fyodor Doestoevski, who, almost prophetically for Joan, wrote so poignantly and intimately about prisoners and prison life. She also read everything she could on Hitler, appalled by his plan for systematic annihilation of the Jewish race. She would often exclaim, "how could the people not rise up in defense of the Jews? How could the people not rise up?"

Joan was 25 years old when seven of the nine men on the Supreme Court legalized abortion. Joan said she thought there would be a great outcry from the pulpits, she thought people would take to the streets. But there was very little done, and the aboratoriums opened for business. Joan's fight against abortion has never ceased since then. Joan and her sister Susan opened their apartment to women that they had saved from entering the abortion mill. Through counseling and "sit-ins," they saved mothers and their preborn babies. Susan told me that Joan didn't sleep anywhere but on the floor for months at a time.

In 1978 Joan and Susan went to St. Louis to join their sister Miriam who was then a student at St. Louis U. In the late '70's, they found Miriam and other students from the university sitting in and blocking entrances to abortion mills. Joan said it was seeing her gentle and tender sister Miriam courageously facing abortionists that gave her courage to do the same. Joan always knew that the horrible violence to the preborn that goes on inside aboratoriums had to be confronted at the abortion mills. This takes courage because direct action at abortion mills means attacks from the abortion personnel, as well as rough treatment from the police. In fighting abortion, Joan knows she is fighting a root evil that denies that all life comes from God. God tells us that all life has a purpose, in joy or suffering. All life has a meaning.

In 1980, Joan lost her right eye to a fiercely malignant melanoma cancer. Joan was told by her surgeon at Bethesda hospital that the cancer could return at any time. Meanwhile, throughout the 80's, she was arrested dozens of times trying to stop abortions. Each jail sentence becomes longer and harder. In 1983, Joan got her first sentence of a half year. It was at Gumbo prison in St. Louis. The harshest sentence, of course, has been the five-year sentence given to her in Pensacola, Florida. . . . I hope she is released in 1988.

Letter from Joan Andrews to Peter Lennox:
13 February 1987, from Broward Correctional Institution
When I was a child.we attended a little country public school called Belfast. Bill, John, Susan, and I were the only Catholics at the school. We transferred there when Daddy got a teaching position and became principal. I was in the

4th grade at the time, though I was ten years old. I did not start school til I was 7 because I wouldn't go without Susan. How my parents let me get away with this, I don't know. Even though Susan was younger than I, she appeared more like the older sister. I was extremely cowardly and shy, to an abnormal degree. To some extent, in the same areas, this is still true to this day. I relied on Susan for everything as a child. I always had her speak for me. . . .

For weeks prior to my transfer from Lowell to Broward, knowing I was scheduled to go, I would time and again wake up in the dark with my heart frantically beating, feeling a strange panic. . . . I kept wanting to get it over with, but when I thought the transfer was imminent, dread would grip me. I cringed at the prospect of the scene I would face at Broward when I revealed I would not be cooperating. People always got a little bent out of shape when informed of this, no matter how nicely and politely you'd say it. . . .

Anyway, the kids at Belfast school had a deep prejudice against Catholics. They believed us all to be liars, cheaters, and, to put it in general terms, just no good. There seemed to be two main aspects to my personality. On the one hand, there was the cowardice and shyness, which forced silence upon me while the teacher would rant against Catholics and Catholicism, a favorite topic of hers; and on the other a strong loyalty and protectiveness for family, friends, and especially the Faith.

Though this latter trait did not overcome my cowardice in front of an adult, it displayed itself with no problem in regards to other kids. Thus I ended up spending my recesses, and often the before and after school periods, in dirt fighting the boys. I rarely fought with the girls as they all wore dresses and I didn't know how to deal with their taunts. A boy, you could wrestle with, or hit. Susan and I were the only tomboys in school and therefore the only girls to wear slacks. Only once did I hit a girl and that was because she made Susan cry. . . .

I can clearly relate to your telling me how you would hide real tears, for I do not cry often, especially not in front of anyone, but even when alone tears are rare. . . . in school, no matter what was ever said or done to me, or no matter how hurt I felt, I refused to let myself cry. When I was in the 5th grade, several of the big boys from the high school who hung around the elementary school while waiting on their school buses, decided they were going to make me cry. It became a nightly ordeal after school each day. They met me out back of the school, alone with Susan, and they'd punch me in the stomach. I, of course, had to prove that Catholics don't cry, nor snitch, so this went on for weeks probably, though at the time I thought it was most of the year before the boys got tired of it and quit. They never did make me cry. However, I recall feeling sick to my stomach with dread each morning and not wanting to go to school. . . . If one of them had dared lay a hand on Susan. . . . I'd have attacked them with all my might, as well as reported them, probably. Certainly if it happened more than once. As it was, they seemed satisfied to concentrate on me, and I'd just stand there and look at them trying not to show any emotion at all as they'd give me a good half dozen or so punches each day. I don't know if this explains why to this day I have such a problem being able to cry. Sometimes I feel tears coming on and then something inside clamps down. I regret it, but I seem to have no ability to counter this. It makes me feel like I'm being cold around people because I can't cry freely. And I've been accused of this a few times. In recent years it has bothered me so much that I prayed asking the Blessed Mother to teach me how to cry.

Well, it doesn't really matter anymore. Inside, I can cry, and maybe do it more than I should these days. What matters is that God knows how each and every one of us feels, and whether we can cry or not, He cries for us. What a God we have!.... By the way, I have mostly good memories about Belfast school and the children and teachers there. In time, after the first couple years, many good friendships were forged. As it ended up, we all started getting along beautifully, and there wasn't anyone I didn't like. The one particularly hostile teacher never changed, but then she probably couldn't help it. Most likely she was raised on the prejudice she so vehemently expressed....

Peter, whether or not you are able to get me out of here, you have already made the biggest rescue as far as I'm concerned, that of my spirit. Of course, God did it, but you and Dana were willing to be His instruments, His holy vessels, in my need. Your sister always, in the love of Christ.

To Richard Cowden-Guido:
4 November 1987, Broward Correctional
During childhood my main interests were Jesus and the Faith, my family, the farm, horses, and also reading (horse stories or lives of the saints. Horses won out on volume, but being a very slow reader, I never read 'volumes'). My mother instilled us with a love for the Faith from our earliest memories. When I was a preschooler, I wanted to be an Indian, and lamented that our family wasn't a little redder in skin-tone.

More and more as I got near my pre-teens I began to develop a strong interest via revulsion in the Nazi holocaust. And I developed a deep desire to know how one should respond to any given situation morally—as God would want one to. So I read and watched TV programs with these questions in mind.

During high school, [I had only] a little civil rights involvement, though I became very involved in opposing the Vietnam war. Not in demonstrations, as there were none around my environment in Nashville during those years, from 1962 to 1966. It rather took the form of debate and prayer. At college, there was some civil rights involvement on a minor scale, though in the spring 1966 semester I became very involved in anti-war protests, fasts, and prayer. But I became disenchanted with the anti-war group on campus and left it and school after that one semester. I also left because I was emotionally distraught because my brother John was drafted during that semester.

I lived at home with my parents from 1966 to 1973. I spent most of my time writing stories, some children's stories, but primarily stories regarding morality. Most pertained to war, though I touched on abortion, about which I had heard, though it was not legal then. I was a rather ignorant, ill-informed individual. I never dreamed until I was hit with it in 1973 that abortion would ever possibly be legalized. I did not even realize that New York and other states had legalized the killing before *Roe v. Wade*!

Also, during this period at home, I worked with horses at the farm, raising them, breeding them, breaking, training, buying and selling them, though I never was a good businesswoman. Never made any money at it. But I thoroughly enjoyed it, and living at home made it possible to have this kind of career with horses.

Of course, my dream was always to one day marry a wonderful, devout Catholic man and to raise a huge family of barefoot kids (hopefully on a farm). But he never came. Of course, I never went out to meet anyone. I contentedly stayed at home and expected God to send the right man to me. I expected him to come knocking on my door.

I cannot express my shock and horror in 1973 with the abortion decision. I awaited the uprising of the Catholic Church, but that did not come. I made plans and preparations to disarm the killing weapons in the abortion centers, and prayed for guidance and strength. In December of 1973 I headed by bus to Chicago to begin this effort, which I expected to become my life from that moment on until the holocaust ended or God called me to leave this life. I did not particularly think of martyrdom, but, not knowing how long the holocaust would last, I knew unless it ended in my life-time I'd be working to end it until the end of my life.

I felt very gloomy that December. I expected to be in and out of jails for the rest of my life, with long, long sentences each time. I am so happy that this is not what has developed at all, and I do not see my small sentences for non-violent rescue "sit-ins" to be the fulfillment of that forecast. I am not at all gloomy now, for back then I never foresaw others, in a movement, confronting the killing head-on, and having comradery, and support. How very pessimistic I was about people! How unrealistically I saw everything. It was as if I would always be all alone.

Maybe that misunderstanding had something to do with why I chickened out after a couple of days in Chicago. But though I abandoned the plan that December in fact, I never abandoned it in my heart. I only decided to postpone it for awhile. In the meantime, I got involved in all the other activity of what soon became clear was a growing movement. I first heard of a rescue (sit-in) at the St. Louis National Right-to-Life convention in 1978. Miriam and I signed up and were overjoyed this action was being taken. We missed it because of a surprise bridal shower sprung on Susan the day of the planned "sit-in."

Sadly, I thought this was a one-shot convention-linked action. I didn't know the real situation. In the fall of 1979, Miriam went to St. Louis University for nursing school, and, lo and behold—there was the rescue movement! She phoned Susan and me immediately to tell us! During that phone call, we worked out a plan where Miriam would relay to us everything about rescues so that Susan and I could organize them in Delaware. All that fall we organized and finally found five people to agree to do a first rescue with us in Delaware and to be members of this initial direct-action Delaware cell, which we hoped would grow rapidly. However, the week of the rescue, everyone dropped out and said they couldn't do the planned rescue and didn't feel they could do a future one. Being so terribly naive and inexperienced, I didn't know a person could do a rescue alone. Therefore, during Advent of 1979, Susan and I decided to pull up stakes, go to St. Louis, and join the rescue movement there with Miriam.

We got there right after Christmas, but the next rescue wasn't until March 8, 1980. That was my first rescue. Then, we organized to start doing weekly and bi-weekly rescues. In May 1980 I lost my eye.

The rest is, well, history. Archbishop May [who came to St. Louis from Alabama—where there is a history of official opposition to sit-ins—almost exactly when Andrews did] came out strongly against the rescues and it was a major factor in strangling the movement in St. Louis, which was the most vital rescue group in the country at that time. Although he didn't really strangle it, only slow it down, for it is still very much alive, and much of my activity has been there. . . .

To her brother John: 23 November 1974

Daddy has been clearing the farm and it gets more and more beautiful. He's also making trails all through the woods. . . . None of the cows had their calves. They're fine, though. There are still ten baby calves—no new ones. Big Mama hasn't calved yet. I love you.

24 January 1979

We have the greatest news! Susan is getting married!!! After three and a half years of knowing and dating David Brindle they are getting married!!!!

It's really great, John. David. . . . will make a wonderful husband and a good father, and he's so very much in love with Susan and she with him. . . . David is such an honest person, I asked Susan why it had taken them so long to get married, especially since she knew he agreed way back to have as many children as God sent them, and that they are compatible morally, and in how to raise children. . . . At the root of it Susan thinks it was her fear they'd have the same problems in religion Daddy and Mama had. . . . David is so much like Daddy. Susan has always loved that, because she loves Daddy so much, but also it caused her doubts, remembering how difficult things were with Daddy and Mama since they were so different in their backgrounds, and because David isn't a Catholic. Those fears are gone now and Susan is without doubt, and simply full of joy and peace.

Father Frank Ruff will marry David and Susan here in Saint Louis at the College Church of St. Xavier. . . . Everybody in the family is so happy. . . . Susan and all the family wish you could come to the wedding. Could you ever, John? [John Andrews was living and working in Saudi Arabia at this time.] Please, please try. . . . God bless you, John. We're so excited and happy. All my love.

[Joan's father was received into the Catholic Church in 1972. David and Susan Brindle have six children.]

20 October 1979

Miriam is having the greatest time at SLU! You wouldn't believe all her friends!. . . . It's a co-ed dorm, and everyone seems really nice. Everyone we passed yelled to Miriam, "Hi, radical," or "Hi, convict" [this letter was written while Joan was organizing the ill-fated rescue in Delaware—after a visit, and shortly before she moved to St. Louis; Joan had never been arrested for a sit-in at this point, though her younger sister Miriam had]. . . .

One of her very closest friends, Sam Lee, was arrested with her. . . . He's so great. You couldn't meet a nicer person, and he's so intelligent! We went to his trial one of the days we were there (he's been arrested four times for similar sit-ins), but he was so brilliant on the stand that the prosecution kept hurting itself by trying to get him to trip up, by provoking him to be irreverent of others—the police or the clinic staff.... But there is no antagonism or meanness in him. And it came through, so the prosecution had to step back.

Sam was in the anti-war movement too. And, of course, is against capital punishment. With his beard and all, he looks like a young Russian intellectual dissident. A young Franciscan named Vince was on trial with him, plus two women in their early twenties. They are all so unusually nice....

Bill and Claudia [Joan's brother and sister-in-law] are having their annual Fall party today—with hay ride, *et al.* And it's a beautiful Saturday for it too! The leaves are changing, and it is just perfect out—balmy, with the leaves drifting down from the trees.... Clarence is going with me to the Horse Auction tonight because we're selling one of the horses, a two and a half year old which has been well trained. It'll be fun.... Got to go. God bless you, John. I love you so much.

26 November 1979

We are all so worried about the situation over there. I know Saudi Arabia is normally very stable, however so much is happening all around it, and after the crisis at Mecca, we are all very uncertain and worried. John, please take care of yourself. We wish you could come on home. Please think about it....

Well, I'd better go now, John. Susan and I are in such a whirlwind of events and preparations right now. We took in another young mother and her three children, all aged under five, into our one bedroom apartment, and we must find them housing before we leave Delaware. Whew! They won't let them stay at Red Mill because she's on welfare, has no job and no husband.... God bless you, John. We love you so much.

To Dana Lennox: 4 February 1987, Broward Correctional

My Dad wasn't a Catholic, and the three girls, like our mother, always deeply loved our Faith and Jesus. I think the boys did, too, when they were young. Years later, my brother Bill told me he lost his faith while he was in Vietnam. He found he could not believe that a loving God existed Who would allow such evil. He told me of some of the things he saw, and it was indeed grotesquely evil. John . . . wanted to believe in Jesus, but was intellectually made to feel it wasn't true. John still goes to Mass often, and he feels a sadness and a loss, I think. David simply lost his faith, pretty much the same way. . . . Each of my brothers is a very caring and charitable person. . . . And how they suffer without the joy of Christ. Dana, the little prayer you said for me as you closed your letter was so utterly beautiful and most deeply comforting. . . . May God overwhelm you with His presence. . . .
In His Love.

To her brother John:
22 March 1980, two weeks after her first rescue

John, I know you would love it with Miriam and me here at St. Louis University. We have such great friendships. You wouldn't believe all the fun we have. . . . Mike is always arguing philosophy with Jane, who is working on her doctorate in philosophy. Poor Mike, it seems we always gang up on him, even though he never actually opposes our viewpoints;

it's just that he sees shades of distinction in arguments where none in substance exists; whereas others are more direct, giving credit to reality. A distinction which makes no difference is no distinction. That which contributes to an end is part and parcel to the reality. Of course, the importance of good philosophers is to be able to see when a distinction that doesn't seem to make a difference really does, or will. Anyway, we have so much fun. . . . God bless you, John. I sure love you. Please come home soon. All my love.

10 April 1980

The sit-in actions are beginning to produce some amazing results. While we were sitting in at the city clinic, Janie was invited into the abortion doctor's—Escobido's—office, because he wanted to hear what she had to say. We had the clinic closed down by 10 a.m. Escobido had four patients who came—then none. Usually he has 35 or 40 patients on Saturday. His asking to speak with Janie was. . . . something no one could imagine him doing. He always sneaks in and out the back door escorted by police.

Everyone—especially the police—was shocked. He told her she looked like an intelligent woman and he wanted to hear what she had to say. When she first got into his office he kept saying that he could tell she was very intelligent, as if that were very important to him. Then they talked. For an hour and a half they talked. Janie had been a little scared to go in so Escobido allowed one of the young men to accompany her.

Escobido at first tried to justify what he did but Janie brought it down to brass tacks, and Escobido then admitted he knew he was killing human beings. "But you must understand, it is legal to do it," he said.

Janie then pointed out that he was very dark-complexioned and that at one time that was all it took some people to feel they had the right to take another's life. As for legality, the property/non-person status of Dred Scott was just one well-known example of legal injustice. She told him it was people like those outside the clinic who defied such laws, and changed them, by risking their lives and livelihood to secure human rights for all races. Now we want that to extend to all ages—all age groups.

Escobido just gazed at her, then said: "I think you will do it. You will change the abortion laws. Eventually, you will." Then he said, "You have been praying for me for a long time. I know it."

The nurse came in twice telling Escobido that the girl in the procedure room was ready (one of the four who had gotten in). He kept putting her off, saying he wanted to talk with Janie. Finally the nurse was insistent that he had to come now. Escobido got up and asked Janie if she'd wait til he got back. Janie came apart. She said, "You want me to sit here and wait til you go in and kill that baby? I can't believe this. No, I won't. I won't wait here."

After a moment he asked Janie for her phone number, saying he needed to talk to her more. Dick, the young man, gave his name and number too. The nurse then starting cursing Janie and Dick, and pushing Janie to get her out. But Janie went over to Escobido and put her arm around him and said, "If ever you need me, or want me to come, I'll come. Just let me know."

On the way out, Janie stopped in the waiting room, seeing a girl waiting for an abortion. Janie went right to her. The nurse starting yelling, Escobido looked incredulous, and Janie told the girl her name, told her why she was there, and asked her to leave with her. The girl told her to go to hell, and several police took Janie out, but not before she got in a few more pleas and handed the girl some Birthright literature.

The police didn't arrest Janie, since she had been invited in by Escobido. She then sent him a message to ask him if he'd see a priest. He said yes. A priest went in and talked to him for about a half an hour. When he came out he told us he couldn't tell us much because of confidentiality, but he asked us to pray very, very hard. Escobido makes thousands of dollars a week doing no deliveries, only abortions, so if he is about to make a decision, it may be a hard one. Please pray, John!

The S.W.A.T. team handles our arrest and removal now in the county, since our intervention actions have grown so large. Every week we are met with seven to ten police cars and usually three paddy wagons—which make more than one trip sometimes. Being a tactical force, they usually handle hostage situations, sniper situations. Our actions give them a chance to relax more or less. They are coming to speak more and more of their support for what we are doing, many of them. They all like Sam Lee. It's hard not to like Sam. They don't even drag him out anymore, they carry him. There's a definite change going on.

In our sit-in in the city this week, the police read us Miranda. First time for that. We were also charged with resisting arrest as well as trespassing. They don't charge that in the county anymore—despite passive resistance. The city police also search us. They did strip searching once, but our lawyer hit the roof—now just partial. The city does things differently than the county.

I haven't described the Vigil yet. It was magnificent. It started Friday evening. It was very cold, but 300 people showed up. There were candles in paper bags lining the driveway and parking lot to the clinic. It looked like a small Lourdes—300 people in a continuous procession in front of the clinic carrying candles in styrofoam cups. After the service ended, an Extraordinary Minister led a rosary. After the rosary, most everyone left—except the forty or so who stayed for the all-night Vigil. . . .

The big news of this week is a $1.1 million suit filed by the owners of the building housing Regency Park Abortion Clinic. . . . twenty of us have been named in person, including Miriam and me, but everyone who has ever been arrested for trespassing at Regency Park is also a defendant. Michael Gibson and Joe Koterski have an appointment to see the newly installed Archbishop of St. Louis—John Lawrence May. He has forbidden priests to sit in. They want to change his mind. Miriam had an hour interview last week with Father Fizgerald, head of the Theology Department, concerning Charles Curran teaching at the University for a summer course. Curran teaches abortion is sometimes OK, plus other things.

At a recent meeting Tim Finnegan mentioned he hoped his trials would all be over before summer so he would not have to stay in the city indefinitely, and Jerry Murphy, one of the lawyers, said, "Don't concern yourself with that—you may be in jail all summer." He added that actually we could end up serving a year in jail for the offenses with which we're charged. It is possible, but not real likely. Then he said with a smile, "But what's a year for the cause?" . . .

You know, it's really unbelievable how the abortion business, not just the abortion mentality, is very intertwined with the fabric of government, which is so pervasive in public health agencies and government sponsored programs concerning health education. Janie told us how she investigated abortion businesses in Chicago and dug into their tax situations. She dug deep and discovered they were not paying a fraction of the tax money they should have been paying out to the IRS. She got the documentation and brought all the evidence to the IRS, but the IRS agent told her to forget it. She was naive and laughed. Then he really scared her. He put it to her that she was in deep personal danger. He told her to drop it. He said that he didn't want to see her get hurt, but that she had no idea what all she was getting into. He reiterated that it was too big for her to handle. Besides that, there was nothing she could do. He told her to walk away while she could. This was in Chicago.

Janie went home and told her Dad, and he told her immediately to drop it all. That "her friend" in the IRS was warning her about organized crime. Janie obeyed her father. Janie's father has worked in the government for years. . . . he works for HEW now in D.C. He seems often on the verge of losing his job because he won't OK programs that promote abortion or birth control. . . .

Miriam and I really hope we get home this summer. . . . Well, I'd better go, John. I sure love you. Please take care. God bless you. Love.

[Archbishop May has continued his defense of the abortion industry's right to function unhampered by sit-ins; and, according to Joan, Dr. Escobido is still an abortionist.]

10 July 1980

Dave is really a wonderful person and a fantastic husband!! Susan is really happy. Miriam and I have been having a great time. We have another 11 days here but I wish it were longer. The baby is due the day after tomorrow, on July 12. I can't wait! I hope it comes on time.

The last time I saw my doctor [in May, Joan had had her right eye removed due to cancer], he told me that the completed report had come back from the pathologist, and that it was good. The type of melanoma stayed the same all the way through—which is very good. It could have worsened. The cell type is a much less grave type than had been suspected by my doctor and the others. So I'm in great shape. From this point all I need to do is to see a cancer specialist, solely as a precautionary method, twice a year, though I'll have to do that for the rest of my life.

Did I tell you that Miriam and I are working with Mother Teresa of Calcutta's order? They have a house and three sisters in St. Louis and we have begun working with them. It's wonderful—we love it!

John, I'll end now. But I'll write as soon as Dave and Susan's baby comes, with all the information. I love you so much, John. God bless you. Love.

[The cancer went into remission, and though it could return at any time, it has not done so since the operation.]

28 November 1980

How can I thank you enough for your marvelous letters! Oh John, I appreciate so much your telling me your feelings and opening yourself somewhat to me. . . . And John, concerning your comments about your reaction to the elections, I don't feel bad. I have a view of priorities that is pro-life, because that involves issues and down-to-earth policies that will save or destroy the most lives—those of unborn children, the mentally and physically handicapped, and the aged. Stopping the killing to me takes a priority even to the other programs that aid the poor. Because to kill the children of the poor through abortion is the worst crime against the poor, I want the political figure who would allow that out of office first; then I'll work on making the pro-life candidate consistent in his values, when he is inconsistent.

John Ryan says it is the liberals, the Democrats, who have betrayed us, betrayed their own philosophy, because they should be the ones who are prolife, for it follows their other humanitarian stands. It's their consistency that is all fouled up. John is totally liberal on all other issues—totally anti-war, anti-capital punishment, 100% for programs assisting the poor, the handicapped, etc. . . .

I understand your feelings about Reagan. In fact, I

know many a pro-lifer who found they could not vote for
Reagan, but since they could even vote less for Carter, they
wrote in a candidate, or voted for Ellen McCormick. But
many prolifers had a hard, hard time voting for Reagan, and
did so only as a priority of issues, a lesser of two evils, like
the abolitionists—to abolish the evil of slavery, other good
issues had to play second fiddle or else they knew they'd get
nowhere. . . . Although I do feel Carter is a little less hawkish
than Reagan, he was almost as ready to get us into a war
over petroleum, and actually said so. I don't trust any of
them. . . .

I really like the pictures you sent of yourself! I sure do
love you. God bless you.

2 December 1980

John, you can't imagine how thrilled Miriam and I were
with what you said about wanting us to join you in Europe
for "a vacation to end all vacations." Miriam and I will get
our passports just in case it could work out, but you'd best
leave it up to us to get the airplane tickets because if this
fantastic plan does come off, it will necessarily have to be at
the last moment. This due to our trial dates and the real possibility that we'll be serving some jail time shortly. We'd have
to work our trip around that. So let us get all set up for it,
and if it works out from our end, we'll let you know. Gee, it
really would be the greatest though! . . .

Bill cares about his own men behaving morally, cares
about his country doing what is right, and even says if one is
a soldier in the midst of a war and discovers his country is in
an immoral war, he is obligated to refuse to fight. No question about it. You can't continue to participate in an immoral war just because you are a member of the military and
are under orders to continue fighting. Bill's a very faithful
person and he's faithful to his Catholic Faith first. So I do
know what a good person he is. . . . I know he always cares

about his enemy as a human being, a child of God. . . . And yet, John, it would be terribly hard for me to marry someone who would carry arms, or be involved in wars or killing. At the gut level, I abhor all war so much, and though some people adhere to the just war theory, how truly often do we fight wars in self-defense, or the defense of others?

John, it's really difficult. Horrible, in fact. And yet, it is true I do really like Bill. He's such a gentle and good man. He called the other night and asked if he could see me, so this Saturday he's coming down to spend the day. He was so nice over the phone. I've never talked to anyone quite so nice. Well, whatever happens, I hope God blesses him. . . . God bless you, John. I love you so very much. I'll write again soon.

2

News Story, The Philadelphia Inquirer: 11 October 1981

Joan Andrews has been arrested 45 times in the last 18 months for blocking the doors of abortion clinics. As a result of her protests, she has suffered a broken finger and has spent 15 days in jail. She and her sister, Miriam, two of six offspring born to William and Elizabeth Andrews of Lewisburg, Tenn., credit their devoutly Roman Catholic parents with instilling in them the strong religious beliefs that they say have led them to follow their course of protest.

"We've been brought up very strong in our faith," Miriam Andrews said. "We were taught that it always comes first. You never deny it."

Joan, 33, is the third oldest of the six siblings; Miriam, 22, the youngest. When Joan was 12, her mother had a miscarriage during the third month of pregnancy that played a crucial role in forming Joan's views on abortion. "He was only three months along, but he was perfectly formed," Joan recalled. "He was born here in the kitchen. We had the ground blessed, and he was buried in the yard. . . ."

Miriam has been arrested 65 times at St. Louis protests. Neither has been convicted as a result of any of those arrests. According to Joan, the protests work. "One day, we turned away seven women. Five went to a pro-life center, and the other two took our literature and said they would reconsider. It's very effective. Every week, we turned away two or three women who said they wouldn't have an abortion."

When Joan Andrews arrived in St. Louis . . . she began going blind in one eye. . . . [A] doctor told her she had cancer. . . . She went in for the operation to have her eye removed on a Wednesday and was back in an abortion clinic protesting by the next Saturday. . . . Joan Andrews joined a protest in Baltimore that led to her first conviction and jail term. On Aug. 8 [1981] she and nine others were arrested and charged with trespassing. All were convicted Aug. 31 and Andrews was fined $300. She refused to pay and was sentenced to 30 days in jail in Baltimore City Jail. Ms. Andrews and another woman involved in the protest were put into a cell with women charged with crimes ranging from murder to prostitution. . . . During her stay, Ms. Andrews was infected with lice. . . . On Sept. 14, halfway through her sentence, she was released. . . .

From Joan Andrews to her brother John: 26 July 1981

Yesterday, Saturday, Miriam and I sat in at an abortion clinic in Wilmington—it was Delaware's first abortion clinic sit-in. And we were amazed how nice the police were. Many said they agreed with us. One young officer went over to the abortion clinic personnel and tried to explain why we couldn't move from the door and why we had to do it! Amazing!. . . . God bless you, dear brother. I love you so much. And I miss you, John. Love.

To her sister Miriam: 6 September 1981, Baltimore City Jail

I know I do not need to explain to you why I refused to pay the fine, nor allowed anyone else to pay it for me, though it was offered. . . . I always knew what my response would have to be, but I am even more confirmed in it now, with a renewed sensitivity toward not compromising the dignity of the unborn by such a travesty—submitting to paying a fine, a penalty, for trying to save lives! Our common humanity with the unborn makes this totally repelling. . . . However, I certainly see nothing compromising in anyone else paying their fine, by the very fact that this perspective is so totally individual and subjective. . . .

Jail is pretty much what I expected. It's not too bad, and yet there are times I get a little claustrophobic, and I try to find some sky to look at. . . . The worst thing is the homosexuality. And it's not hidden at all. The guards don't stop it. I guess it is too pervasive for them to handle. It is so horrifying and sickening. Prayer is the only thing that saves me from becoming ill. There are quite a few fights too. You can imagine the hostility—it ripples like a current when ignited, and spreads like wildfire. This morning I awoke to a fight in the adjoining cell cube. There was yelling and screaming and crashing of chairs (we have a few tin collapsible chairs in each cube), and even metal cots banged about. We called for the guards but they were a long time coming. At first they couldn't break up the fight because, even armed with billy clubs, they were afraid to go into the cell. Finally the matron called for help on the wall phone at her station, and the women were put in solitary.

I like most of the guards. I think they really care, and that they try to be as fair as they can. There is a lot of injustice though—coming through the court system. Ninety-nine per cent of the prisoners are black, maybe five or six whites. . . . There is an elderly black lady, about 80 years old, whose bond was set at $400, or confinement for trial, for stealing four chickens at a grocery (I, by the way, think she was innocent). She is the sweetest person, very gentle and frail, always kind and smiling, and always reading her Bible.

She was so confused, and kept asking why they hadn't let her talk at her trial. Her name is Florence, and, thank God, she was bonded by her son the second day she was here. He had difficulty getting the bond, and at first didn't think he would be able to. God must have aided him.

I'd be writing forever if I started citing specific cases. It's pitiful. There are the real criminals, murder, assault, etc., and then the poor souls who are constantly returning to jail because of their wretched lives—abused, and so they abuse, plus drugs, alcoholism, prostitution, and of course, violence. The most touching thing is the number of women who want to pray with Ginny and me. They see us praying quietly, and they come over and ask to pray with us. We are so overjoyed. Miriam, I can't tell you what a marvelous retreat I am having. Despite the horrors, there is such a presence of God. Evil and good are side by side here. And of course, being here in the first place because of our common humanity with the unborn, and the privilege to do penance for the sin of abortion, is a thing of constant thanksgiving. Of course, my saying that Ginny and I have brought vocal prayer to our cell in no way means there was a void before us. I know in the hearts of many of these women there were prayers, or the longing for it—and therefore the reality.

The sad thing is that we're unable to attend Mass at all. We asked Fr. Chuck if he'd say Mass and he said yes, but first we had to check with our chaplain who is a Catholic nun, Sr. Margaret. But she was negative. She gives a Communion service once a week—on Thursday—and said, "we don't want any outsiders, we want to keep our own community."

There it is again, Miriam! Sr. Margaret, needless to say, is more of a social worker than a nun. She puts her emphasis on social needs almost to the elimination of the spiritual. We begged for daily Communion, even by her hand, as the service only lasts ten minutes and she is here full time and there are only a few Catholics. She said she is far too busy to do that. She seems almost disdainful of the idea of emphasizing the spiritual. I mean it, Miriam, her priorities are all screwed up. For example, she knew I was longing to receive the Eucharist and had been looking forward to Thursday. I had not had Holy Communion since I had been here, and it had been four days. Anyway, I had a visitor, and was sent down to the visitor's room. I had no idea at the time. Ginny [who also refused to pay the fine] begged Sr. Margaret to have me notified so I could attend, but Sr. Margaret said no, that I needed the visitor more than I needed Communion. Her exact words! I was so upset when I found out upon returning to my cell—realizing I had missed Communion for the whole week! We are allowed visitors three times a week but we receive Communion only once a week. The fact is, Sr. Margaret was going on her priorities and feelings. She could have at least asked me.

Really Miriam, the modern and liberal nuns and clergy have become harder and harder to bear. I always try to be charitable externally, but, Miriam, inside I'm in turmoil. I do not accept things as well as I should. It makes me angry. But reading Teresa of Avila is helping me a great deal.

I'd better end this letter soon. I want to tell you one thing more than anything else, Miriam. It is that I am quite sure you and I will probably end up serving a jail term together sometime, and though I dread your seeing the homosexuality and perversion (though you know it exists as I did) I am looking forward to us sharing together the privilege of serving God and doing penance together for the sin of abortion. I am making a marvelous retreat, but if we were together it would be doubled or tripled in its magnificence! God would protect us and we would protect each other.

There is nothing for you to worry about my being here. God does protect. I want you to know just how close we are by telling you something. Miriam, the second day I was here,

I accidentally got put alone in a big isolation cell away from the other prisoners because my bed in the cell cube I had been assigned had not been vacated. They stuck me in a cell alone. Shortly later they stuck in another prisoner to isolate her, forgetting I was in there. And I was never so scared. I knew nothing about her, but suddenly I knew. She was huge, too, and I knew if she tried to touch me the guards probably wouldn't hear me scream for them—the outside halls are so noisy from the prisoners calling out from solitary and the large cell cubes on down. And no guards were around. If she had tried to touch me, she would have gotten a fight like she never expected, but I could tell how strong she was, and I actually trembled inside. Miriam, we must have been together for over an hour—seemed forever—and I managed to get her so involved in talking about herself (with the help of God, Who surely had control of the situation) that I kept her at bay 'til I saw a guard and I quickly got taken out. Oh, Miriam, I was so scared, and my insides were turned upside down at the proximity of perversion. It was only my fear, and my body being prepared to fight that kept me from being sick on the spot. . . . Miriam, I don't want you to think I'll be running into another close call like that. Everything is safe where I am now. The reason I told you this is to show you how important it is to trust God when you are in jail serving a sentence.

Do well in your nursing. I'll be in St. Louis soon. I am longing to be with you. Oh, Miriam, I have gotten a great idea about the Bridgeport sit-ins, and how I can manage to work it where I can sit in every single day and not be a burden on the people who have been bonding. I can't wait to tell you about it—soon as I get to St. Louis!

I'll say good-bye now, Little Hogi. I love you so much! God bless you, little sister. Love.

12 September 1981, Baltimore City Jail

I love you so much and I miss you terribly! . . . Let me tell you of a few things that have touched me since I've been here. Early this week a woman, who is here for prostitution—she's 23 years old, a tall, beautiful, slender black girl—came over to my bed at about two in the morning. I was half asleep. She asked meekly if I were awake. I sat up and said yes. She then asked me hesitantly to pray with her. She asked if I'd pray that her husband would write her a letter. We sat on my metal cot and prayed together, asking the Lord to have Cynthia's husband send her a most loving letter, and for the Lord to continually bless their marriage, and lead them to grow ever closer, to protect their love for all eternity as it grows stronger, and for it to be a faithful reflection of their love for God.

The next morning, Cynthia came over to Ginny and me at breakfast and asked us if we could pray. Once she prayed the rosary with us. You can't imagine the feeling! Many of the girls have names they're known by on the street, such as Shorty Moe, Legs, Smiley, Shortcake, etc. Smiley's brother was hanged by a guard at the men's Detention center next door to us. That was this past February and when the guard was off duty two friends of her brother ambushed him and shot him to death. . . .

I must tell you about an experience of a couple days ago. One of the inmates, named Yvonne, is the mother of an 18-month old child. The father had left them for another woman after five years together. She came up to Ginny and me and said we shouldn't be here. She suddenly started to cry, big tears filled her eyes and rolled down her cheeks, and she told us she loved us, and that she prays we get out soon. We were so moved. She has the tenderest heart. She told us we shouldn't always give away our food and should start taking better care of ourselves. We tried to tell her we were, that we were fine, and to please not worry—that we were very, very healthy. Her tenderness just broke our hearts. . . .

Most everybody here is poor and black. There are some people stuck here with a bond of only $35, but because they don't have it, they are stuck here two, three or sometimes four weeks before their trial. Just because they don't have that little bit of money. Even being stuck here for a day due to an inability to come up with $35 seems so unfair. Definitely some do need to be here—but the chicken thieves, or the lady who spits on the sidewalk too near a parked police car, that's bad. And being dragged in for some minor infraction, just because they are street people, which often it boils down to—it's hard. . . .

Lisa and I were talking about couples preventing children, and Lisa told me that when she knows a couple who only want a certain number and the wife is pregnant and they are hoping for a particular gender, she always prays that they get the opposite so that they'll be open to getting pregnant again. I told her that's exactly what we do!. . . . Well, Hogi, I'd better say good-bye. I love you so very, very much! I can't wait til we are together. God bless you, baby sister! All my love.

To her brother John: 13 September 1981, Baltimore City Jail

We have made some good friends here, and Ginny and I pray often and are making our time into a retreat. There are aspects of jail life that are really bad, and I can hardly wait to get out of here. It almost gets unbearable. But we do have prayers, without which I couldn't make it. There is a lot of ugliness one must turn from. There is also violence. However, the guards are fine women, and I have a lot of respect for them, unlike the guards at the men's jail—which is part of our complex. . . . There is a lot of tension over there. There is tension over here too, and violent eruptions, but they are most often between inmates, not between guards and inmates—though those occur too.

Ginny and I are safe, though. I don't want you to think we are in any danger. Psychological strain is the main burden for us. And never getting out into the open is getting me uneasy and claustrophobic. However, the other prisoners really love Ginny and me. It's strange. They come up to us and ask to pray with us, and they tell us their life stories. They even sometimes cry and tell us they love us. So there is no danger for us. And of course, Ginny and I are together. . . .

In the men's prison there are 1500 prisoners. Last week I got a letter from a man at the Maryland Penitentiary. . . . He's been in prison for twenty years I think. But he spent eighteen years at a Maryland prison called Patuxan, I think. It was closed down a couple of years ago after an investigation which showed up weekly murders and lobotomies besides other atrocities. Anyway, this inmate wrote me because he had read an article about Ginny and me going to jail for trying to save the unborn, and he told us he admires and supports our efforts, and is appalled at the killing of innocent little children. He said that even though society looks at him as a criminal and social outcast, he reacts the same as any other human being in the face of abortion. He told me he wrote a poem especially for me, and he enclosed it. He, however, said that he disagrees with our decision to go to jail; that we should let the men do that. He asked us to please take care of ourselves, and assured us that he was praying for us.

I'll say good-bye now, John. I sure love you and miss you terribly. Please come home soon—to stay. I only have two more weeks to go here. I sure would like to introduce you to Bill! And see you meet Lisa. . . . before I head back to St. Louis. We could have such a nice welcome home for you: with Dave, Susan, Annie, the new baby, Mama and me still here, and Bill and Lisa. We could spend the day on Dave's sailboat. This is a gorgeous time of year. Even brother David may be heading home and passing through Delaware at the same time you arrive. I wish! God Bless you, John! I love you so very much.

5 November 1981

It's strange. This loneliness only draws me to a desire to be more removed. To go further away from everybody. I know these feelings won't last forever. And I don't even really mind, though it makes me restless and sad. I do wish I could be free of the sit-ins here in St. Louis so I could take off. Somewhere beautiful and fresh and close to nature and winter. Somewhere alone, with a cabin and a fireplace I keep thinking. I want to enjoy the solitude. Maybe you feel the same way. Maybe deep down I know why you stay in Saudia Arabia and won't be coming home at Christmas, not til June—nor maybe not even then.

Well, I had better go. It's 9 a.m. and I want to see Joe before Mass. It's a beautiful night. Very cool and windy—with scatterings of clouds. John, please take care of yourself. I love you very much!

19 November 1981

Today a dear friend, Fr. Jim Danis, was buried. I attended the funeral Mass and then went out to the Bridgeton abortion clinic. . . . Fr. Danis had been arrested for intervening at abortion clinics many times. He was the first priest in the St. Louis area to do so. The police once tore all the ligaments in his thumb when he refused to walk out of a clinic and leave the door to the procedure room unblocked. He was a deeply concerned priest, and just as equally gentle toward the women who came to the clinic for abortions. He had a marvelous smile, and he smiled often. I recall his warm personality at the times we got together to plan strategy and times we got together just to relax and relieve the tension of our endeavors. He was a remarkable man.

He came down with cancer about six months after I

did ... [H]e lived for about a year after that, in and out of a coma the last few months. He was conscious and lucid, speaking with members of his family, days before he died. From a robust 200 pounds, he was down to 100 pounds when he died Monday night, November 16. ... I knew Fr. Danis was dying for a long time, but just seeing him in the coffin, slender and black-haired, with his pro-life rose on his chasuble ... I suddenly recalled the warmth and dedication of the man I had seen so often at the clinics. I was also moved I guess because I have been in a strange mood for several months now, feeling lost and lonely. ...

And Fr. Danis was healthy when they discovered my cancer, which they thought at the time was terminal. (Dr. Hoy, you know, thought the remission of my cancer contrary to prognosis, and bluntly told me, as if he thought it slightly shocking, that it was "uncanny," and "unfathomable"). ... Life really is strange. I recall that the main sorrow and regret I felt when I knew I had cancer and the doctors warned me that it was very likely terminal, was that I had never been in love yet. Never known what it was to be held by a man I loved, and who loved me. And then two months later. ... And what developed from that I thought was real ... but it was not. But at least I have known love, and I have been held. And maybe that's enough. ... But I want to have my own children so very badly, and I am getting older and older. Please pray God sends me someone whom I will fall in love with, and he with me!! ... God bless you, John. I love you so very much. Take care of yourself. You are always in my prayers. Please keep me in yours. Love.

26 January 1983

First of all, I want you to know that I am not in jail! I only had to spend two days in jail, then I was allowed to be released on a *writ of habeas corpus* while the appellate court makes a ruling. Since we were sentenced for what they said was contempt of court, we would usually have no recourse to appeal; and in fact, the judge had us jailed and held without bond. However, if a defendant is sentenced to anything over six months, he has a right to a jury trial, which is what the appellate court is deciding now. . . . the court can either reduce our sentences to six months and forego the opportunity of offering us a jury trial, or else it could just offer us a jury trial—and we'd begin all over again. Needless to say, we hope we are offered a jury trial!

My time in jail wasn't too bad, and in fact one police officer sneaked a rosary into my cell. He wasn't even Catholic, but he managed to get it from a fellow officer. When I was being booked, earlier, that same officer apologized for having to book me, and he said he thought it was despicable that we were being sent to jail for trying to save lives. The contrast is great between various police officers. Later in the week when I was arrested at Bridgeton for blocking doors at an abortion chamber, one of the arresting police officers went into a rage when I refused to walk out, and he locked me in a strangle hold by the neck and demanded I walk out. He kept choking me and almost got hysterical. Finally he just dragged me out because I wouldn't submit. He cursed and raged all the way back to the station. I always remain silent in the face of rage unless I am asked a direct question.

My throat and jaw was bruised for more than a week. Having faced this particular officer and others like him before, I think it is an inability for them to accept a disregard for their authority, which of course they don't have in this area. We are always polite with the police, but we obviously cannot accept or acknowledge their authority to force us to leave a death chamber while we are trying to rescue the victim; and some officers are just not able to accept that.

And you know, I am not surprised that many officers do not acknowledge the humanity of the preborn, and I'm not surprised that there are those who, though they do realize children are being legally murdered, yet follow orders and feel it is their duty to stop our rescue attempts. And so I can't be surprised either that this makes many of them, probably the majority, act in an unprofessional and hot-headed manner. Especially I am not surprised by this when you consider that though there are many, many people in our society who are opposed to abortion, knowing it kills our youngest children, there are also many of those who do little or nothing to stop the killing, not even by casting a pro-life vote, or publicly voicing a pro-life opinion, because they are afraid of being viewed unfavorably by friends and peers. So one can understand why police officers behave as they do. Which is what makes officers like Dave Buford, who gave me the rosary, and officer Fitzgerald, who broke down and wept after arresting John Ryan and Miriam, so wonderful. . . . I love you so very much, John, and I miss you terribly, as we all do. God bless you, John. Love.

5 February 1983

Thank you for all your many, many letters. I can't tell you how much they mean to me, but I am sorry you thought I was in jail all that time! That was really sweet of you though, to try to write me every day. You did an amazing job!. . . . As you already know, Miriam has not returned to Christendom College. With the wedding only three months away, she felt it best to have the free time to just plan the wedding and prepare herself spiritually. Also, she wanted some time with Daddy and Mama before beginning her new life. This is going to be a special time for them.

John, please don't worry about Daddy and Mama being lonely or worrying about the kids. They are so very happy together and complete in themselves. Of course, when Bill was going through his roughest period, they were worried about him, but that has passed to a great extent. I wish you knew how truly contented and happy they are. . . . God bless you and keep you, John! I love you so very, very much and I really miss you.

To her brother David: 7 July 1983, St. Louis County Jail
I received your wonderful letter and package this afternoon. You're such a good writer. . . . David, I agree with your thoughts about martyrdom and the giving of one's life for another, but only to a point. . . . To throw away one's life is an offense against oneself as well as against God. . . . [If it is only] an act to bring about an end to life and tribulation, how could this possibly please God?. . . . but removed from that distorted arena, I believe there is to be found legitimate acts of "martyrdom" if you want to call it that. . . . A man who sees God's pleasure in his living, rather than his dying of his own design, and who realizes his mission and purpose is to live as God gave him life, such a person may sacrifice his life for another.

I suppose going to jail for a cause or as a result of prosecution emanating from an outlawed rescue attempt on the behalf of a persecuted segment of humanity could be seen as a type of martyrdom. Forfeiting one's freedom. I don't know, David.

I don't think all people are called by ... their conscience ... to do certain acts of self-sacrifice. We all have different callings, different vocations. It's for the individual to decide, as long as the individual does not deliberately violate or persecute another group or individual. I do not think anyone can decide for him what sacrificial deeds he must perform. . . . We are all told by good will and the Commandments that we cannot do evil, but the performance of good acts is dependent on one's free desire, and should be dictated by love.

Therefore, I can only speak for myself. I tried to rescue a few particular infants being brought to an abortion chamber where they were to be killed, because I would not be

happy if I closed my eyes to it and undertook the more de-
tached work, in the political arena. Personally, it would be
very difficult for me to respond less directly in the midst of a
holocaust. Not that other roles are less important or less vital. I am simply doing what I feel I should be doing. I try to
think about it clearly, and I pray about my actions and my
decisions.

It made me happy beyond words when two women were
reached by what we said, and responded to our offer of assistance, and decided to allow their babies to live. Maybe I'll
see those children some day. This took place at the enjoined
clinic. One such child, saved from abortion, is probably going
to be a very close friend of [Susan Brindle's children] Annie,
Andrew, and Daniel because the mother has grown close to
Susan, and the children play with each other even now. Like
Oli's friend, whom you told me about; sometimes people
touch each other's lives in ways which totally change them.

So, I am not unhappy, and I really do try to take care of
myself and enjoy life. I certainly do not believe God is
pleased by our misery. He wants us to be fulfilled, whole-
some and happy. That is what I want for myself and I know it
will please God. I feel peace with my life David. Not satisfied, but peace. I have many areas I need to work on, and I
have a lot more to learn. I hope I'll keep growing all my life,
despite periodic set-backs. But I hope to be getting better. I
refuse to worry about it, though. My aim is to simply keep
trying. . . .

I miss you a lot, Dave. . . . I'm so glad you're my
brother! I love you so very much. God bless you. Love.

To her brother John: 14 November 1983
Maybe you have already heard but, if not, let me tell
you the great news! I'm being released from jail the day after
tomorrow (Nov. 16) [after some six months]!! I'll stay in St.
Louis for three days to see friends, but will head to Philly on

Saturday morning the 19th. . . . At any rate, I do plan to be at the farm for Christmas! It will be so great to see you then! We'll have such a great time! I can't wait to see you, John! We'll have a marvelous Christmas!! I love you very much!

City of St. Louis Board of Alderman Resolution 152
WHEREAS, January 21, 1984 marked the final day two of four area citizens were released from jail for their violation of a 1980 court order prohibiting interference with the operation of Abortion Clinics, and

WHEREAS, these four (4) defendants were earlier found in contempt of that order and given the following sentences, namely: John Patrick Ryan. . . . 225 days, Joan Andrews. . . . 225 days, Ann Lamb O'Brien, mother of three. . . . 314 days, Samuel H. Lee. . . . 314 days

WHEREAS, the week of their final release marked the eleventh (11th) Anniversary of the United States Supreme Court's decision authorizing legal abortions, and

WHEREAS, strategies of protest expressing moral outrage as a method of Civil Disobedience have prevailed since introduction in America by the late Dr. Martin Luther King Jr.; reflective of a simple idea that decent and concerned people must publicly object to, confront and informationally inform persons openly pursuing the sanctioned injustice.

NOW THEREFORE BE IT RESOLVED the Board of Aldermen, cognizant of the issues above, aware of the price these good people have paid to confront this social cancer that is permitted to spread among us, do by the adoption of this resolution state and affirm to them, that they are not alone in their opposition to abortion on demand; they should worry not, but be of good cheer, for their essential position is true—murder is murder and the commandment remains "Thou Shalt Not Kill"—and all pronouncements and rhetoric to the contrary notwithstanding, that simple fact remains, and their testimony of protest reflects this deep and abiding realization by many of their fellow citizens and countrymen.

Introduced this day by: [Aldermen James Signaigo; Albert Villa; James Shrewsbury; Samuel Kennedy; Timothy Dee; Joseph Beckerle, and Alderwoman Geraldine Osborn]. Attested by: Chief Aldermanic Clerk Jacolyn L. Rolf and Thomas E. Zych, President, Board of Aldermen. The Common Seal of the City of St. Louis.

From Joan Andrews to Diane Bodner: 25 October 1984

Orlando, Florida. . . . The week I have been here has been good. Miriam and I have been getting in a lot of talking amid the work she does at the Crisis Pregnancy Center and sidewalk counseling. There is still plenty of time for being at home, watching John play sports and praying the rosary every evening with a group of Philippinos on the base. They have such a beautiful faith! I'll hate to leave at the end of another week. I am scheduled to go back to St. Louis to intervene again on All Saint's Day, but I may postpone that until I have heard how things are going at Wilmington General in Delaware. Remember, the situation of the hospital policy of killing late term abortion survivors despite a state law which demands care for live-born survivors? However, if the time isn't right for an intervention there since Delaware Right-to-Life is trying to force the State's attorney to correct the situation by investigating and prosecuting, then I might try to get to Tennessee for my parent's 40th Wedding Anniversary in November.

Wish you, Tom Herlihy, Kathy O'Keefe, and Joe Wall could make it to the farm for Christmas—but at this point I don't know if I'll be in jail then. It's a nice thought, though, to dream of a great Christmas all together! By the way, Diane, the date between Martin Harvey and Mary Sainz went very well—despite it being diverted for an hour and a half by a Direct Action meeting I had to attend on the spur of the moment. We all attended, and then cut out as soon as we could and resumed the date. We had a great time, and Martin and Mary hit it off fabulously! . . . God bless you, Diane! Love.

1 April 1985, Montgomery County Detention Center
At this point it does look doubtful that I'll be getting out. Well, if we can't do it for Easter, maybe another time—OK? . . . The inmates have the Georgetown-Villanova basketball game on. I hate rooting for Georgetown, that den, but better than Villanova after the recent rottenness there. I meant to let brother John know that I was supporting Memphis State over Villanova a day or two earlier, but I haven't written John yet. . . . [B]e sure to wish your dear parents a very happy Passover for me. It was really wonderful the times I stayed at your home. Your parents are so very nice! . . . Anyway, thank you for putting up with me Diane. Love.

11 April 1985: Montgomery County Detention Center
Diane, I am so happy that you recorded Wallenburg! I was dying to see it, but my wishes were overruled by the majority of my cellmates. The vote was 15-1, not that it's very democratic around here. Usually it's whoever gets to the set first, or whoever has the nerve to switch channels, or whoever can outshout the others. So I begged off making a fuss, only because I am so nice and considerate you understand. But at your house, it was Wallenburg, right?. . . . Don't cut your beautiful hair! I love you, Diane. You're an angel. God bless you.

To Linda:
1 July 1985, Delaware Women's Correctional Institute
God **bless** you Linda. I know what a sacrifice it took for you to embrace jail when you have the sole responsibility for your young daughter. And yet you placed your dear Jeanine in Our Blessed Lord's hands. What faith and trust that took. Your example overwhelms me. How truly Jesus knows your love for Him. I met your wonderful daughter this past Saturday when Susan brought her with her own children to visit me. What an angel! And you know, Linda, your little girl was so proud of you. You should have seen the smile that spread on her adorable face and lit up her eyes when she told me where you were and why her mother was in jail! Words are sometimes not heard by the young, but an example is the truest teacher. I think Jeanine knows what love of God means! . . . 'Til we are all together again my love and prayers are with you each.

Presentence Report of the Adult Probation Office of the Court of Common Pleas Criminal Division, County of Allegheny [Pennsylvania] (signed by Peter H. Townsend, Presentence Investigator, Adult Probation Services; approved by Ronald L. Boglitz, Supervisor, Presentence Unit) prepared for Honorable Raymond A. Novak: December 24, 1985
Complaint Name: Joan Andrews
   MN: Elizabeth
Age: 37
Birthdate: 3/7/48
Sex: Female
Race: White

Criminal Complaint Number (OTN) and Offenses:
8505630 (B 505232-0)
(1) Criminal Trespass
(2) Defiant Trespass
(3) Criminal Mischief
(4) Resisting Arrest
Plea: 11/6/85—Pled non guilty.
Verdict: 11/12/85—Found guilty of (1) and (2), not guilty of
(3) and (4).
Co-defendants: Joseph P. Wall and 13 individuals whose
charges were handled at the magisterial level.

DETAINERS OR CHARGES PENDING:
1. Anne Arundel County, Annapolis, Maryland
(1) Trespassing on Private Property
(2) Destruction of Property
12/18/85 - Trial continued indefinitely
2. Montgomery County, Pennsylvania
Criminal Contempt.
No trial date. Bench warrant lifted.
3. Philadelphia County, Pennsylvania
(1) Failure to Disperse
(2) Disorderly Conduct
(3) Defiant Trespass
Arrest Date: 10/19/85
4. St. Louis County, Missouri
Trespassing
On docket for February 6, 1986
5. St. Louis County, Missouri
Peace Disturbing and Trespassing
Next Action: 1/15/86
Trespassing
Failed to appear and a warrant was issued

6. St. Louis City Ordinance
   Trespassing on Private Property
   Issued 9/11/85
7. Brentwood Missouri
   12/5/84 - Warrant issued.
   Failure to appear.

OFFENSES:

On May 10, 1985, the defendant entered the reception area and examination room of the Women's Health Services, Inc., located on the third floor of the Fulton Building in Pittsburgh, PA. The defendant continued to remain in an examination room of the Women's Health Services, Inc., despite the fact that she was given notice to vacate by Pittsburgh Police officers.

According to Pittsburgh Police records, on May 10, 1985, police received a call concerning disorderly demonstrators at the Women's Health Services, Inc. Upon arrival, police were met by an administrator, Virginia Shannon, who told police that numerous people forced their way past the receptionist and located themselves in six examination rooms, refusing to leave. Reporting officers yelled through the closed doors for the occupants to leave, but the occupants yelled back that they would not. Police phoned for assistance before they unlocked each of the examination rooms by using a pass key. As police unlocked the various examination rooms, most of the actors refused to leave the rooms. Police eventually forced all of the actors, with the exception of the defendant and the accomplice, out of the various examination rooms. In order to force the defendant and the accomplice to vacate the room that they occupied, police had to break down the door, as the defendant and the accomplice had barricaded themselves within.

According to Virginia Shannon, an administrator at the Women's Health Services, Inc., the defendant and followers make a consistent pattern of their lives by causing disruptions at various clinics that perform the same services as the Women's Health Services, Inc. in Pittsburgh. Ms. Shannon stated that the defendant and followers have been very disruptive to various abortion clinics throughout the country, and what they do is basically take the law in their own hands. She stated that she is aware of the fact that the defendant and the accomplice are very dedicated, but she believes that the Court must impose limitations upon the activities in which the defendant and followers engage. She stated that she believes that, while their activities in Pittsburgh area have been very limited, they have been quite disruptive to Planned Parenthood centers in the Philadelphia area.

The defendant is a member of a group that calls itself the Pro-life Abolitionists League. She is very serious about her beliefs and has devoted much of her life during the past 12 years to involving herself in what she calls her pro-life work. Her convictions are so strong that the defendant had indicated that she cannot accept probation, if a condition of the probation requires that she not trespass at abortion clinics.

The defendant states, by her own estimate, which she believes is quite accurate, that she has been arrested 105 times between 1980 and the present for offenses similar in nature to the present offenses. The arrests have been concentrated in six states, with most of the arrests being in St. Louis, Missouri. She believes that she has been arrested at least 50 times in St. Louis for charges of summary trespassing or contempt of court. During many of those arrests, numerous other individuals who share the defendant's beliefs were also arrested. The defendant stated that the most time she served in the St. Louis area was six months; most of the charges were dropped.

The defendant takes pride in the fact that the objective of their group is to save lives. During one of their protest demonstrations, she stated, they talked nine women, who had gone to a clinic to have an abortion, out of having the abortions.

Concerning the present offenses, the defendant and thirteen others, four from outside of the Pittsburgh area, went to the Women's Health Services, Inc., an agency that regularly performs abortions. They locked themselves in examination rooms and they remained there until police arrived; everyone, with the exception of the defendant and the accomplice, was removed without incident. They barricaded themselves in the examination room and sufficient force had to be used to remove them. The defendant stated that her group's intention was to save another life, a goal they feel that they accomplish even if they simply shut down an abortion clinic for one day.

The defendant has given up everything in order to participate in what she calls her life's work. She has no possessions and the only clothes she has belong to a sister. The money that the defendant receives is derived from donations she receives from individuals who share her same convictions.

PRIOR RECORD:
Adult:
The defendant has been arrested approximately 67 times in the St. Louis area for charges such as summary trespassing and contempt of court. A thorough examination of the arrests indicate that the defendant has never been convicted on the misdemeanor or felony level. In fact, the record of most of the 67 arrests has been ordered expunged by one court in that area. Almost all of the defendant's arrests were for violations of municipal ordinances, for which the maximum sentence was 30 days in jail.

On three occasions, the defendant was charged with violating restraining orders, forbidding her to trespass at various Planned Parenthood centers, and she was found guilty of contempt of court. She was ordered to serve terms in jail of 20 days, 45 days and 225 days; she served one day of the 225 day sentence before being released.

Police in Bridgeton, Missouri, where most of the defendant's St. Louis arrests have occurred, stated that the defendant and her followers are totally dedicated individuals, who, because of their beliefs, have indicated that they will not comply with the law. None of the people arrested was considered violent or destructive, and they were described as non-violent pacifists.

According to one source interviewed, an assistant county counselor in St. Louis County, the prosecutor in that county has absolutely refused to criminally prosecute people arrested for their pro-life beliefs.

As far as can be determined, the defendant has been convicted on the misdemeanor level on several occasions, which are noted below.

Date and Place	Charges (Indictment /Complaint Nos.)	Disposition
7/14/84 Rockville MD	Montgomery County Circuit Court Docket # 035395 Trespassing on Posted Property	4/24/85-Guilty. Sentenced to 90 days in the Montgomery County Detention Center, all but 66 days suspended; given credit for 24 days; eodie, placed on 2 years' unsupervised probation.
4/11/85 Rockville MD	Montgomery County Circuit Court Docket #010345D-0 Trespassing	5/20/85-Guilty. Placed on 1 year probation.

The defendant has never been supervised concerning this probation, as authorities in Montgomery County, Maryland, were going to transfer the defendant's case to Newark, Delaware, where the defendant was residing with her sister. The defendant spent 28 days in the Montgomery County Detention Center before being placed on probation for this case.

6/15/85	Municipal Court City	7/25/85 - Found guilty
Wilmington, DE	of Wilmington M-85-	(see below).
	06-1051 Criminal	
	Trespassing (2nd Degree Misdemeanor)	

Addendum to Presentence Report
Correction to arrest as noted on April 11, 1985:
When the attached presentence investigation was completed, authorities in Montgomery County Circuit Court in Rockville, Maryland, indicated that on May 20, 1985, the defendant was placed on one year's probation. Authorities in that County checked further into this case and learned that the defendant refused to sign the probation contract, as did numerous other pro-lifers, who were placed on probation at the same time. The court, in turn, dropped the probation order, and gave the defendant credit for time served in the Montgomery County Detention Center, which was believed to be approximately 28 days.

The defendant received a suspended prison sentence and was placed on probation for one year, with the special condition that the defendant not return or engage in demonstration activity within a two-block radius of the 1200 block of Orange Street. The defendant was further ordered not to engage in demonstrations in any residence connected with persons in the 1200 block of Orange Street.

6/15/85 Wilmington, DE	Municipal Court City of Wilmington M-85-06-1053 Conspiracy (3rd Degree Misdemeanor)	7/25/85-Guilty. Suspended imposition of imprisonment, with 2-year probation, to run concurrent with M-85-06-1051, with special conditions mentioned previously.

Probation authorities in Wilmington, Delaware, remembered this case quite well, in that 40 pro-lifers were placed on probation the same day.

Family History:

Relation	Name and Address	Age	Occupation
Father	William Andrews Louisburg, TN	70	Ret. Teach.
Mother	Elizabeth Andrews Louisburg, TN	68	Ret. Nurse
Siblings	William Andrews Santa Fe, TN	40	Coll. Prof.
	John Andrews Franklin, TN	39	Lawyer
	Susan Brindle Newark DE	36	Housewife
	David Andrews Knoxville, TN	28	Student
	Miriam Lademan Anapolis, MD	26	Housewife

Other Significant Information:

The defendant was born in Nashville, Tennessee, on March 7, 1948. She is the third of six children.

The defendant's parents are second-generation farmers. The defendant was raised in the same home that was once occupied by her grandparents.

Following her graduation from high school around 1968, the defendant attended college for one year at a university in St. Louis, Missouri. After leaving school in 1969, the defendant returned to her parents' farm, where, for the next 10 years, she worked at a thoroughbred training center on the farm, raising and training horses for racing purposes.

According to the defendant, following the Supreme Court decision in 1973 that legalized abortions, the defendant became heavily involved in what she calls her "pro-life work," which has continued to the present. When the defendant became involved in what she also called her "life cause," she left home around 1980 and supported herself by working part-time as a horse groomer, working at various race tracks.

When the defendant was arrested for the present offenses, she was living with a sister in Newark, Delaware. The defendant has no possessions and little money for support. Most of her income is derived from other pro-lifers, who give her money.

The defendant's sister, Susan Brindle, also a pro-lifer, stated that she is very close to the defendant and shares her beliefs. She stated that she and her husband provide a home to young women who are pregnant and have no place to go. She stated that she is very proud of the defendant, who has given up her life for the unborn. Ms. Brindle further added that the defendant is a gentle, loving individual, who truly committed the present offenses out of her love for the unborn child. She remembered an occasion when they were both young (11 and 12 years old) when the defendant jumped into a swift-moving river and saved a cousin who was drowning. The defendant could not swim at the time, but was determined to save the cousin's life.

MARITAL HISTORY: Single; Children: None

Other Significant Information: The defendant has never been married, but she indicated that she would very much like to marry and have children in the near future.

HOME AND NEIGHBORHOOD:

When released from jail the defendant will reside.... with her sister, Susan Brindle. She has lived there for three years.

Since leaving home around 1980, the defendant has not maintained a permanent residence.

EDUCATION: Graduated from high school and attended one year of college.

RELIGION: Affiliation: Catholic (Active)

Other Significant Information: The defendant stated that she attends Mass daily when she can find the time. She does not view her involvement in the present offenses as a religious issue, but described her involvement as a human rights issue. She believes that it is her moral duty to save lives, and she has committed herself to saving the lives of the unborn babies.

HEALTH: Height: 5'5"; Weight: 120; blue eyes; brown hair

Other Significant Information: At the present, the defendant stated that she enjoys fairly good health. In 1980 she lost the sight in her right eye due to cancer (malignant melanoma).... According to the defendant and her sister, this type of cancer can return at any time and in most cases is fatal. The defendant was fortunate that they found the cancer during a routine check-up. The defendant should be checked routinely for any possible recurrence, but she has been somewhat lackadaisical in following through with these check-ups.

EMPLOYMENT:

The defendant has no employment record to speak of, because of devoting her life to what she termed "saving the unborn." During the past several years, she helped her sister and her husband as a counselor and coordinator at the home that her sister runs for unwed mothers. The defendant did not receive any pay for this employment. Aside from earning small amounts of money by training horses and by donations the defendant has received from supporters, the defendant has no income.

EVALUATIVE SUMMARY:

The defendant, a 37-year-old female, is making her initial appearance in the Allegheny County Criminal Division, on the charges of criminal trespass and defiant trespass. The present offenses occurred when the defendant came to Pittsburgh from her home in Delaware to take part in a pro-life demonstration at the Women's Health Services, Inc. She and 14 other followers barricaded themselves in the examination rooms, disrupting services and necessitating their forcible removal by police.

The defendant described her activities as a moral obligation to save the unborn child. Authorities at the Women's Health Services can appreciate the defendant's beliefs, but not what they call taking the law in her own hands. The defendant and her followers have disrupted Planned Parenthood centers in several states, causing considerable difficulty in the Philadelphia area.

The defendant has been arrested approximately 105 times for offenses similar in nature to the present offenses; the present offenses have resulted in her first felony conviction. She currently awaits trial for several other cases, and she is in violation of several probations as well.

The defendant has indicated that she will not accept probation if it will "limit my pro-life work."

From Joan Andrews to Father Paul Quay, S.J.:
6 January 1987, Broward Correctional

Father Quay, when you asked if I could calculate how many days I'd spent in jail, and to put the calculations into segments according to different jails and areas, I didn't know if you meant jail terms only; or if you wanted me to include days spent in jail on days of arrest, before being released on ROR [released on recognizance] bond. So I'll generally state that I have been arrested about 120 times, and have spent usually an average of six hours in jail on each of those days. About sixty or seventy of those arrests took place in St. Louis, primarily at Manchester, Bridgeton, and University City, though some were in the city as well. The other arrests were scattered between about six other states: Maryland; D.C.; Delaware; Pennsylvania; New Jersey; and Florida. Interestingly, I have been arrested the least number of times in the state of Florida, being just one time. These arrest days will not be included in the calculations below. As for the jail terms themselves, either awaiting trial or serving sentences, I've roughly figured the following:

St. Louis: 221 days total. Five in St. Louis City Jail; 6 in Bridgeton; 75 in St. Louis County Jail; and 135 in Gumbo.

Washington D.C.: 4 days total, in D.C. City Jail.

Maryland: 64 days total. Fifteen in Baltimore City Jail, 46 in Montgomery County Detention Center, 3 in Annapolis's Anne Arundel County Jail.

Delaware: 44 days total. Two in the Wilmington City Jail, and 42 in the Delaware Women's Prison

New Jersey: 10 days total, in the Camden County Jail.

Pennsylvania: 85 days total. 8 in Delaware County Prison, 6 in Bucks County Prison, and 3 in Lancaster County Prison, 4 in City Jail, 30 in Philadelphia County Prison, and 34 in Allegheny County Jail (Pittsburgh).

Florida: 261 days total. 163 in Escambia County Jail, 43 days at Florida State Prison at Lowell, 55 at Florida State Prison at Broward. . . . and counting. The total number to date, all inclusive, is 689 days.

[Counting roughly 26 full days of the six-hour stints not included in her report; and the 353 additional days she served at Broward since writing the report; and 27 days at Alderson Federal Prison in Alderson, West Virginia; and 40 days in Delaware Women's Correctional Institution where she now resides (as we go to press on 1 March 1988): Joan Andrews from the August/September 1981 incarceration described in her letter above, has spent some 1,135 days in jail: or three years, 40 days.]

Letter from Donna Cordingly: Undated

It was four years ago this past May when I first met Joan Andrews. I was pregnant and scared, confused as to what to do with a baby I didn't think I had any way to support. I was single with one child, no job, and struggling to make ends meet. I am not proud to say that an abortion had crossed my mind. I told a friend of mine how afraid I was and she pleaded with me to talk with a pro-life counselor. . . . Dr. Isajiu . . . put me in the hands of a woman in Delaware. Little did I know the loving hands of this remarkable woman would guide me through the best decision I ever made.

This gentle woman with genuine and deep heart-felt concern . . . went to work with a zeal to help me get on my feet and help me to support the life I, with her urgency, had decided to spare. I had never met a person with so much compassion and commitment to befriend another human being. I know it is that benevolence that showed through that made me first listen to what she had to say, and that saved my child and me from the horror that could have taken place.

My daughter is now four years old. I thank God for her every day. To think that I may have never known the warmth of her smile, the joy of her personality, the love she brings to me, is a pain I am glad to say, I will never have to know. . . .

If there is ever a doubt about Joan Andrews, her motives, her purpose, remember me and my daughter. . . .

Reflections by Juli Loesch: December 1987

I first met Joan Andrews in 1985 in Pittsburgh, Pennsylvania when, along with about a dozen other people, we were arrested for blocking the door of an abortion clinic. I had heard a few things about her, formidable things. Joan's done 100 sit-ins . . . they said. Maybe 150. Joan never cooperates with the cops, they said. She doesn't pay bail. She fasts in jail. I thought: Spare me. . . .

The activists had a brief planning meeting at a Burger King about a block and a half from our target. Women's Health Services is the Abortion Pentagon of the tri-state area: about 10,000 women come into this place every year for the Procedure. . . . Joan, a plain-faced, poorly dressed woman—37 at that time—said nothing at this tactical meeting. I didn't hear a peep from her during the 2 hours when we were blocking the doors to the Procedure Rooms. I can't tell you whether she sang or prayed aloud, as most of us did, or if she spoke to the clinic personnel, the soon-to-be-aborted teenagers, or the police. And when we were hauled off the premises and ended up at the police lock-up—3 bare steel holding cells, four women per cell—I lost sight of her altogether.

After ten hours' wait, I was, I thought, the last one to be called out for the bond hearing in front of the magistrate. All the other women were released on their own recognizance.

"Since you're from out of county," I heard the magistrate say, "we are imposing a $100 cash bond."

"I . . . haven't got it. . . . "

"Then you are remanded back to the custody of the County. Matron, take her back to her cell."

When a whole group is being jailed, there's a wonderful esprit de corps: "Singing or Non-Singing Section?" the Matron had chuckled as she escorted us to our cells. But now I was alone. To my humiliation, I recognized the onset of my old claustrophobic terror. My heart pounded; I broke out in sweat; I experienced a choking, suffocating sensation. I had the insane desire—and if you've never experienced a phobia, you won't know what to make of this—to tear off my clothes and batter myself against the bars.

The Matron peered in at me. "You're really in distress, aren't you, honey? I'll put you over here with your girl-friend." And she transferred me into the cell with Joan Andrews.

Now I felt wretched shame. What did I expect this formidable woman to say? (You haven't even spent one night in jail! Get a grip!).

"Joan," I said, "I'm sorry. I feel so weird." She sat down next to me and put an arm around me. "You're shaking. You feel like jumping out of your skin. I know." Taking both my hands, she began a Rosary—as I realized a few Sorrowful Mysteries later, when I was calm enough to understand the words.

"Are you thirsty?" she asked me. "Here, take this." She handed me a halfpint of milk and a sandwich: her portion of the lunch the rest of us had wolfed down five hours before. "Didn't you eat?" I asked. . . .

It calmed my inner turbulence to hear her clear, gentle voice, so after the Rosary I wanted very much to keep her talking. I kept asking her questions about her life. Obedi-ently, Joan answered. She grew up in rural Tennessee, south of Nashville, pitching hay, picking fruit, and milking cows. . . . Her father William has a law degree, but he didn't like ar-guing ("Imagine such a lawyer!" she laughed). . . . her mother had a miscarriage. The children all were shown their tiny brother's delicate body. Into the box which was lovingly made for his burial, each of the children placed a lock of hair. . . .

"My two favorite things ... are horses—and—match-making!" She shot me a glance and laughed. I suddenly noticed how pretty she was.

"Do you want to get married? And have kids?" Yes, she did.

"Do you have somebody special?" Sadness. No. Not exactly. There was a man she cared for, but he wanted her not to rescue babies anymore. "Do you have somebody special?" she asked. "Aah. . . . Sort of. No." Her face grew bright with merriment. "Specify. What kind of guy are you looking for?"

"Are you serious?" I laughed. [She answered] "I've already matched up ten friends—five couples—and I'd love to do the same for you!"

By this time, we were both giggling like 15-year-olds. What kind of guy? How many cubic feet? If he were a dog, what kind of dog would he be? If we were dogs, what kind of dogs would we be? Am I a setter, a pointer, or a retriever? Would I like a Great Dane? Or a so-so-Dane? If I were a spaniel and my husband were a beagle, we could have a Spiegel. And go into the catalog business! We were helpless with silliness, holding our sides, when the Matron came to the cell door with an announcement: "Miss Loesch? You can go now. Your buddies outside have raised your bond."

"But I don't want to go," I gasped. . . . "You go," said Joan seriously. "You're not ready to refuse bond. Maybe you will be someday, but not now." And without a hint of reproach—or any reference to the fact that I was leaving her alone in the cell for God knows how long—she sent me on my way. . . .

She was never convicted of much more than trespassing. Until Pensacola.

Several abortion facilities had been bombed in Pensacola, Florida, in late 1984. The streets, the clinics, were empty, and nobody was endangered or injured. But when two young couples, local born-again Christians, were arrested for the bombings, the extended public drama of their trial and conviction had a chilling effect on the whole pro-life movement in Pensacola [as well as on insurance rates, which prevented two of the gutted centers from ever re-opening].

"It's like, people were spooked," said one local activist. "They didn't want to do anything. No picketing, no sidewalk-counseling. People were afraid if they even wrote a letter to the editor against abortion, their neighbors would say, 'Are you one of those bombers?'" Joan could sympathize with the defendants' goal of "actually stopping abortions and not just talking about it." But she was deeply concerned to show the world that you can "actually stop abortions" through nonviolent action.

On March 26, 1986, after having informed the police and the abortion staffers of her intentions, Joan Andrews entered an empty, unoccupied procedure room at the Ladies' Center, [the only remaining] abortion site in the city of Pensacola, and attempted to unplug the electrical cord on the suction abortion machine. She was immediately seized by the police (who were on site waiting for her) and went limp upon arrest. . . .

3

Report in the Pensacola News Journal: 23 July 1986

In a decision that virtually eliminated the possibility of a state prison sentence, an Escambia County Circuit Court judge Tuesday found Joan Andrews guilty of burglary of The Ladies Center, but not guilty of committing an assault during the burglary. . . . If, at sentencing on Sept. 24, Anderson stays within Florida Sentencing Guidelines, Andrews will face a maximum penalty of 364 days in county jail [the Guidelines' maximum recommendation in fact is 12 to 30 months]. If the judge also had found her guilty of assault, the guidelines would have called for a maximum penalty of three years in state prison [though in fact life imprisonment is the maximum].

To Diane Bodner: 23 April 1986, Gumbo Jail

I just called Tom May and found out that his mother had died yesterday morning. God bless her. I wish I could make the funeral this Saturday, but as soon as I am released, the city will pick me up on a warrant. Tim Belz got money from Earl Essex to post both my county bond and city bond so that I can head to Florida at once. I must turn myself in to the Escambia County Jail in Pensacola because the judge revoked our bonds there when we picketed the killing center after our hearing last Thursday. I did not hear of it until yesterday when my Pensacola lawyer got hold of me. The people who posted my $20,000 property bond risk losing it unless I turn myself in by Friday at 8:30 a.m. Thus I am forced to post bond in St. Louis in order to get out of jail here. Tim Belz says we will get the bond back, and that he'll fight any confiscation!

Diane, we missed you at the Christendom spring formal. Damien Caruso said he would have loved to be your escort but for the short notice. Another terrific fellow, Jack Saunders, also really wanted to go. God bless you Diane. Will write more soon.

30 April 1986, Escambia County Jail

I'm doing well. Really, I'm pretty used to jail by now, and am just "biding my time." I had the great joy today of being able to receive Our Lord in the Most Holy Sacrament. So you know I am doing just fine. Diane, you are in my prayers, as always, and very much in my heart. . . . Can't wait to see you again. God bless! All my love, in Christ and Mary.

9 May 1986, Escambia County Jail

I just last night received your very enjoyable and entertaining letter. Oh, but Diane, please don't torture me by saying those things as though I'm some sort of saint. Come on, Diane, you know me and you know I'm no saint. I go to jail from time to time, and that certainly doesn't make me holy (I wish it did, I'd just stay in jail). You're such an exasperating friend. But I sure am glad I am your friend. . . . I love you, Diane.

17 May 1986, Escambia County Jail

Laura Dunn wrote me that Police Chief Kleinnecht was

exonerated of any dishonorable behavior in his accusations against prolifers in St. Louis. She started to feel upset, but then remembered that as Christians we cannot expect to be loved or to receive justice; that Christ said His followers would be hated and rejected because though in and for the world, they are not of it. That as He was persecuted, they also would be persecuted.

The Catholic chaplain here has a problem with prolife and prolifers. He thinks we're pretty despicable, it seems. Please keep him in your prayers, that God will soften his heart to the plight of the preborn children, and enlighten his mind. You have to feel sorry for him, because he has such a deep antagonism. I can't understand it. But he needs our help, our love and our prayers.

You asked about the Pensacola case: Well, there's not much to tell. Four of us went inside the chamber and disarmed the murder weapon. We all got out eventually on bond (pretty steep bond: $20,000). Then when our hearing came up the prosecutor tried to get a condition put on the bond saying that we could not go out to the mill at all. . . . The judge refused to put this condition on the bond, but warned us against going there and causing an incident. Karisa and I went out and picketed after the hearing, and the judge revoked all of our bonds, after siding with our attorney at the hearing and only warning us against an incident. There was no incident, but our bail was revoked for picketing legally. That's it in a nutshell. . . .

Sweet dear Diane. You don't need to send me anything. God bless you. I have my rosary and a breviary, the mercy of God devotional, a Bible, and the Stations of the Cross. And I'm afraid they wouldn't allow me to accept a big bag of M & M's or chocolate kisses. . . . Thank you again for your wonderful, wonderful letter. Please know that I am doing well. . . . May God bless you and keep you always, as well as your dear family, and may Our Blessed Mother hold you close.

To her parents: 2 May 1986, Escambia County Jail

I sure love and miss you. . . . I'm doing fine and friends in other areas are trying to help out with this Pensacola case. Whatever happens, I am at peace and am happy to leave it in God's hands. . . .

As far as my own life is concerned, I have come to the conclusion that I am meant to stay single. . . . I must be called to the single life . . . there is one man I knew I even loved right from the beginning, but . . . God has called him to . . . the Holy Priesthood, the highest vocation of all. How deeply God loves him! What a great priest he will make! . . .

I'll say good-bye now. I sure love you, Daddy and Mama, and I'll try to get to the farm to see you whenever I get the chance. I have so much I want to talk to you about. Did I ever send you the Divine Mercy devotional? It's so tremendous. We should pray it many times each day. God bless you, dearest Mama and Papa! All my love in Christ and Mary.

To Joe Wall: 15 June 1986, Escambia County Jail

I pray all went according to God's plan in Denver this week, and I also pray the same for the action at Comly Road today. As I write this, I realize that you may already be in custody at the Roundhouse. God love you!

Joseph you sweet, dear co-warrior. I was able to receive some word of the Denver rescue over the T.V. Heard that 21 were arrested, but scanty details. Of course, heard of Scheidler's arrest on a warrant from Pensacola. That was really underhanded of the authorities. They are so often right in the camp of the abortionists—not in the least unbiased. Evil is so pervasive. I suppose that is the tendency with a holocaust, because so many have to go along with it in order to keep it legal. It contaminates almost everybody. . . .

A friend of mine from St. Louis, Jennie Ritter, sent me 50 rosaries and 50 scapulars. I was able to hand out the 50 rosaries to the female inmates, but since I ran out (there are about 70 of us) Jennie is sending me more. I told the ladies that they could pray ejaculations on the beads since very few know the rosary, but quite a few want to learn the rosary. Since many of these are in other cells, Jennie sent me (they just arrived) 50-100 "how to pray the rosary" cards and these were passed out to everybody. They would not let me keep or give out the scapulars. When I asked if I could at least have one for myself, the C.O. took the scapular off the piece of paper explaining what it was, and handed me the paper. . . . God bless you, dear Joe.

17 June 1986, Escambia County Jail

I ask you to forgive me for taking so long to write to you, but I was without envelopes for a long time, even after I received stamps through the mail. I'm all set now though. Tom sent me a whole manila envelope full of envelopes. . . . I like the pictures you sent of yourself, which you sketched at the close of your letters, Joe. You'd better watch out or I may enlarge them and send them all over the country as you've done with mine. So behave yourself and don't make any hero of me, Joe. . . . God bless you, dear Joe. You are always in my thoughts and prayers. Yours in Christ and Mary.

18 June 1986, Escambia County Jail

Joe, would you clarify one thing? Point out that there would be no problem for officers opposed to abortion-killing to protect abortionists from being harmed, any more than it would be to protect KKKers or Nazis or any other group . . . but where the problem comes in as Catholics, is the difference between protecting abortionists and protecting their killing. When the abortionists are killing children, no Catholic officer has the moral right protect this, even if the state has deprived them of their God-given rights. . . . Yours, in Jesus and Mary.

19 June 1986, Escambia County Jail

I can't wait to hear how your three trials turned out yesterday. . . . I am so, so proud of all of you, and so deeply touched by the courage, faithfulness, and love constantly being displayed as a visible witness for the whole community to see. . . .

Oh, let me share this with you! There is a sign which hangs on the wall in Our Father's House. It reads:

> If you were to be
> arrested for being a
> Christian today, would
> there be enough evidence
> to convict you?

Isn't it great?. . . . God bless, Joe!

To her fellow rescuers: 30 June 1986, Escambia County Jail

There will always be differences of opinion in our rescue work, but this isn't the important thing. None of these differing opinions matter. What is important is how we deal with each other. Are we courteous, are we trusting of each other, do we allow each other to make different decisions than the ones we advance, without making accusations? Do we relate to each other with love?

I, too, am a prime offender . . . giving in to the attacks of the devil, causing . . . the personal attacks going on among us. But we cannot give in to this! Rather than give in to it, it would be better to become a hermit and pray day and night to overcome our own unfaithfulness to each other and to God. By offending God, even if we were to win out on our opinion, even were our opinion, our position, the correct one, we would lose the only thing that really matters—doing God's will in charity and understanding and humility. Please forgive me, because I am the worst offender, as divisive as anybody, but it is wrong. Indeed, we must strongly and purposefully put forth views and positions which we espouse . . . but we must do it in charity, with courtesy and respect towards each other. . . . Whenever we are closest to following God's will, as surely this rescue work is, the more vehemently is the devil going personally to attack each one of us, finding our greatest weaknesses. . . .

Please forgive me for preaching. I certainly haven't been the best example [but] please, please, let's all make a firm resolution never to offend God by lack of charity towards each other. What does it gain us if we win every battle by crushing our friends and foes alike if we deeply offend God? . . . .

I sure love all of you. Please forgive me for my past offenses, and please help me to do better in the future. Be patient with me and remind me to be patient with you when I forget. God bless you! Your co-rescuer and friend.

To her parents: 25 July 1986, Escambia County Jail
The trial went very well. I'm sure you have already heard the news: two life felonies were proven false, and thus I was only found guilty of a third degree burglary, and was acquitted of assault, and then was found guilty of two other remaining misdemeanors. It looks like I'll be here at least until September 24, and I hope I'll receive time served at that time. If not, it will not be an outrageous sentence, as was possible before. All is still in God's hands. Maybe between now and September 24 I will be released on personal recognition bond. It's not likely, but there is always a chance. . . . I love all of you very much. I'm doing fine. God bless you, dearest Daddy and Mama. Love.

To Robert Bird: 28 July 1986, Escambia County Jail

We must stay very close to the Sacraments. I am confident that if we remain faithful despite the hardships and the temptations to act divisively, Our Lord will be pleased and He will bring forth the victory, despite our bungling. Whatever happens, we must rejoice in the knowledge that we serve God's holy purpose by accepting all things and offering it to His honor and glory. Thus whenever we are acquitted and set loose it is a victory, just as it is an equal victory whenever we are convicted and sent to jail, so that we may offer reparation for the sin of abortion, and thus beg mercy and conversion for those involved in the killing. . . . It was an honor to be arrested with you in St. Louis. God bless you and love you.

AP Story by Bill Kaczor, Pensacola News Journal: 9 Aug. 1986

A woman convicted of invading an abortion clinic was kept in jail Friday after she again refused to promise she wouldn't repeat her crime. . . . In rejecting postconviction bail, Anderson said Andrews, who has been arrested more than 100 times in similar cases, was a danger to the community and the victims because it was likely she again would violate the law. She might even miss her next court appearance if jailed in another state, he said, something that has happened in the past. . . . The judge also said she doesn't have any ties to Pensacola and that the only reason she came here was to break the law. . . .

"I'm relieved," said Georgia Wilde, one of the victims, after bail was denied. "I just hope it increases the understanding that the law of this land must be adhered to." Wilde is head of the local chapter of the National Organization for Women. She was working as a volunteer at The Ladies Center when it was invaded. . . .

To Diane Bodner: 16 August 1986, Escambia County Jail

Miriam came down to Pensacola and testified for me at a hearing a week ago for post trial release. The judge denied it, of course, but it was a great treat to see Miriam and Margie and Pam Rayburn, who flew down with Miriam. I am doing fine. I hope no one is worrying about me because I really do have peace. [If I get] time served. . . . I'll rush back to spend some time with Dave and Susan, John and Miriam. I do expect to be seeing you!! So plan on it. I am already cooking up some good times, like going dancing and canoeing and picnicing and all sorts of good stuff. . . . God bless you, dear Diane! Much love.

Letter from Joe Wall to Judge William Anderson:
19 August 1986, Escambia County Jail

Are you aware that Joan Andrews has malignant melanoma, a . . . virulent form of cancer? About six years ago she had her right eye and the surrounding tissue removed because of a tumor resulting from this disease. Since then, she has gone into remission, but the etiology of malignant melanoma is that you are never actually cured, the virus lurks in your system. Sooner or later it returns, and the second bout is invariably fatal. This can mean a couple of years, perhaps five . . . even twenty years, but . . . you will be struck down eventually. As confirmed by Philadelphia physician Roger B. Daniels.

What this means, concretely, is that Joan Andrews [if sentenced to] one, two, three years at the Sept. 24 sentencing hearing . . . may have in effect [been given] a life sentence.

To sisters Susan and Miriam:
26 August 1986, Escambia County Jail

Whenever I am feeling especially claustrophobic in jail, and there is that twinge of panic, I just think back to another time and place. I catch hold of somewhere else and dwell in the happiness of that period ... hopping gray stallion, fighting for his head, breezing down a pasture trail from the highfield to a woodland meadow, known as Saddleback ... or sitting on a rock jetty on the Hudson River between Manhattan and the Bronx, gazing into the clear blue eyes of a slender, flannel-shirted young man, whose quick smile breaks with surprising warmth and humor ... handsome face. ... God bless.

To Susan Brindle: 4 September 1986, Escambia County Jail

Last night, dearest Susan, I learned about your cancer when I talked to Miriam and then you on the phone. Even though it hurts, and it is even scary, I felt your wonder, expectancy, and, yes, joy too, in God's will. I pray with all my heart that your brush with cancer will be as triumphant as mine and that you will live to be an old, old lady of at least a hundred. Longevity is in Dave's family, and therefore you have to remain at his side all the way. Deep in my heart, I believe God wants this for you. Our prayer will be constant, that our will be His will, but I believe it pleases Him for us to ask tirelessly with hope and trust for what we hope His will is. I do this about my desire to marry, as you well know.

I believe this thing has been put into our lives so as to bring us closer to God and to each other, as well as to rekindle our awe for each day and each moment given us. These very words were your loving, consoling message to me over the phone last night. Oh, Susan, thank you for consoling me when I should have been consoling you. I love you so! I respect you so, and I am so proud of you!!. ... Love.
[The cancer disappeared, a medical misdiagnosis]

To fellow rescuers: Undated, Escambia County Jail

I feel deep peace and acceptance for whatever comes. Let others know this just in case the sentence is a heavy one.

There will be a time when the courts will begin hitting us hard. We must be prepared. At the same time we must not shrink back when it comes. We need to pray for strength that we hang together and accept in perfect submission whatever trials and penances come.

Some of us who are single, as myself, may be freer to take on the rougher sentences; however, whenever possible, I think our people should demand as much from themselves as possible. Not that we should demand it of each other, but I hope individually, those who are able will shoulder the heavy burden when it comes. This must be a decison we each make with God alone, and with our families.

Will you spread this message among our people? We need unity so badly, and we also need great sacrifice. I think God will grant us the moral courage to do His work—all we need is trust. And I deeply believe that almost all people, with very few exceptions, are called to the rescue of the children, physically, themselves. But all, without exception, are called to support the work in some way. Amidst a holocaust in one's land, I feel one cannot live a virtuous life without being part of this compelling work in some manner.

To Tim and Diane: 23 September 1986, Escambia County Jail

Thank you so very much for your beautiful letter! It was such a joy to receive. God bless you and Diane, and all of your people who are involved directly rescuing the babies at the killing center where you live!!! I can't tell you how moved I was to read about your rescue! It was magnificent. I just glorify God for all of you. . . . You have made me so happy. . . . With all my heart, I thank you. . . . May God bless you and keep you always, dear Tim and Diane, and may the Mother of God hold you in her tender care. Your sister in Christ and Mary.

[This was written the day prior to the five-year sentence handed down by William Anderson.]

4

Syndicated column by Joseph Sobran: 28 November 1986

It's hard to believe that if she had actually broken into a house and stolen a TV set, she'd have gotten five years. But Miss Andrews was trying to prevent abortions from being performed, as is her habit, so the judge threw the book at her. . . .

Miss Andrews is serving her term in a maximum security prison [in fact, medium security, though she was at maximum in Broward by the time this column appeared] in Lowell, Fla. She is a surpassingly gentle woman, single at the age of 38 . . . but the other inmates are tough, violent lawbreakers, and Miss Andrews has been told that she will be lucky to live through five years in the place. It's that violent. . . .

The judge who did the sentencing justified the stiff term by observing that Miss Andrews was "unrepentant." She would neither promise to stop doing "rescues" nor pay any restitution to the abortionists. Granted, we want criminals to display contrition, and this mitigates our desire to punish them. But all this rests on the assumption that the positive law and the moral law are in alignment. Murder is both wrong and illegal. We expect the murderer to repent.

97

But what if murder were legal? Would someone, then, who interferred with a murder by illegal means be expected to "repent" in order to receive clemency? . . . Joan Andrews is evidence that an immoral law can't be workable. Legalizing abortion has made lawbreakers out of otherwise law-abiding people . . . but when such people act on their convictions, the legal authorities are expected to treat them as criminals, to incarcerate them with hardened criminals, and even to sentence them more harshly than criminals are usually sentenced. . . .

It is grotesque for an agent of the state to demand of her a display of conscience. Joan Andrews has shown her conscience in acts of courage and sacrifice. The state has shown no more conscience than an abortionist. It is her prosecutors and judges who should repent.

To Dr. T. D. O'Brien: 27 September 1986

Three days ago I was sentenced to a five year state prison term. . . . I think my family knows that I was prepared for a pretty heavy sentence, though my lawyer and most of our activist leaders did not expect it. Having gotten to know Pensacola judges, I must admit it did not come as a great shock, though I had thought a lesser sentence was more likely. At any rate, please let Pat and Russ and everybody who may ask know that I am doing very well. The Lord is so very good, and He has blessed me with deep peace over all of this. In fact, I rejoice in it because I know God will use it to strengthen His people at work for the salvation of souls and to end the holocaust. . . .

Dr. O'Brien, I hope you and all the family are doing well and are constantly being deeply blessed. Please know that all of you are very much in my prayers. May the Lord bless you and keep you, and may Mary our Queen and our Mother hold you and the family tenderly in her care. With love, in Christ and Mary.

To her parents: 28 September 1986, Escambia County Jail

I sure love all of you and miss you, and know how much you love and miss me too. But please know what peace I have concerning this prison sentence. Please experience the same peace, as I pray you do. Just realize that I am going to use this time as a very special retreat. . . . Dear God is so good and gentle. He is taking good care of me, as I know He is taking good care of my family and loved ones too. Through this, He will bring about much good! So please be joyful with me, please be as happy as I am. I'll see you as soon as I get out, and I'm not worried when that will be. . . .

May the Lord bless you and keep you, my dear Daddy and Mama, and may Mary, our Queen and our Mother, hold you in her tender care. I love you with all my heart, Daddy and Mama, John and David, Bill and Claudia. . . . My dearest family! Love always, in Christ and Mary.

To Earl and Kathleen Essex:
28 September 1986, Escambia County Jail

Be consoled in the knowledge that God is protecting me and all our people, in or out of jail! Maybe you might feel it was more my doing than God's will that I ended up with this prison term, but that is not really the case because I had no choice but to speak the truth. I could not allow the judge to even try to give me probation, community control, a fine, or restitution. You understand this, don't you? I think you do. Therefore, it was unavoidable from my end.

Anyway, please be happy. I don't want you sad. I love you both so. We'll still have that evening of the VHS movie I want to show you—The Big Country—and popcorn and so-das, and ice cream too!! It will be so much fun! Please give everyone my love, and let everyone know I'm doing just great. I'm in good hands, just remember how gentle God is! . . . May the Lord bless you and keep you and may Our

Lady be your comfort, as she was for the child Jesus. All my love, in Christ and Mary.

To Joe Wall: 22 October 1986,Florida Correctional at Lowell

In Disciplinary Confinement, I cannot have commissary use, nor phone use, nor visits (except attorney), nor rescue books, etc. So you see, that's how it is. Please let people know so they don't waste time and money mailing me something like a book, or try to visit. The prison will not allow it. In fact, my mother came to see me, but it was not allowed, despite the fact that she had driven from Tennessee, over a thousand miles away. Luckily, I got to see my brother, John, because he's a lawyer [working on the case]. . . .

Please know that I am praying for all those whom you asked me to pray for. . . . Be sure to always fill me in on the good news of engagements and births and marriage among our friends, as you always do. Also deaths and illnesses so that I can pray for specific people. I think you especially know how isolated one can become behind bars, so I certainly appreciate this. . . . God bless you, dear Joe. You are in my thoughts and prayers always. Take care of yourself. In Christ and Mary, Love.

To her parents:
24 October 1986, Florida Correctional at Lowell

I am sorry that I was not allowed to have a visit with you, Mama, when you came to the prison with John. But I did have a wonderful visit with John. John and I are so very close and I am so very grateful for this. I hated to see the visit have to end.

When I was being brought back to my quarters, I tried to look for you, Mama. I was able to see part of the parking lot from the walkway the officer took while escorting me back, but I didn't see the family car, nor you. . . . However . . . to think of you being only a few yards away. So close. I said my rosary when I got back to my cell and asked God to give you and John a safe trip home.

Please don't worry about my weight.... John can tell you how well I look. I look the same as always. In fact, I was weighed by the officer in charge of the Confinement area just today and I weighed 117. While at Escambia County Jail before my fast I weighed 122, and I expect I'll be back at that weight before long because I have been eating normally except for my two days ... per week, and this won't make any difference. Many, many people do it in accord with Our Lady [Queen of] of Peace's request that we take on sacrifices. She specified this fast as one means [and] ... when I was confined in the infirmary during my straight fast, the doctor told me I was in great health. In fact, I had all my exams which were due yearly. So please know how well I am physically. Oh, and one other thing, I do drink liquids during my Wednesday and Friday fasts....

I sure love all of you so very, very much, and you are constantly in my thoughts and prayers. God bless you and keep you and may the Mother of God hold you close to her Immaculate Heart. All my love.

Report in Pensacola News Journal: 22 October 1986

An Escambia County Court judge Tuesday refused to reduce the five-year prison sentence he imposed on anti-abortionist Joan Andrews for burglarizing The Ladies Center during a protest last March. But Judge Anderson left open the possibility that he would consider modifying the sentence [all the others arrested with Joan had been released more than two months before] if Andrews promises to obey the law, something she previously told both the judge and the probation officer her conscience prevents her from doing.

"I was hoping you were going to come here today and say Miss Andrews had changed her mind about what she's going to do with her life," Anderson told [her] defense lawyer . . . who filed a motion asking for the sentence reduction. . . .

In September, Anderson doubled Florida Sentencing Guidelines and imposed the five-year sentence. . . .

"She and many of her supporters skip around the country spewing their hatred rather than doing something constructive. . . . It's a shame Miss Andrews has chosen to waste her life in prison instead of accomplishing something," Anderson said.

Letter to Law Professor Richard Stitch:
31 October 1986, Florida Correctional at Lowell
When I was a child I wondered how such a thing as the mass murder of a segment of people could take place in any society without the good people in that society stopping it. The strange thing is, as an adult now and seeing it with my own eyes, I still cannot understand how it is happening. Not that I am responding as faithfully as I should. That's part of it. I cannot understand how I have been so weak in most of my efforts. . . . Your sister in Christ and Mary.

Letter to Father Tom Cusack: 6 November 1986, Lowell
God bless you all for your love and concern for me. I think you know how deeply it touches my heart. It is a great consolation to be so cared for, especially by someone so dear as you, dear Father. Thank you for always looking out for me, no matter how far away I am.

At the same time, I don't want you to feel bad about my situation. I realize it is much easier on me than it is on you and my family and my friends. I realize how I would feel if the situation were reversed and you were in prison. I don't think I would handle it very well—even knowing what I know of the joy and peace that comes of at least trying to do God's will, however faltering and clumsy that attempt may be. But know that God is really richly blessing me daily, and that to be in your prayers makes me feel like a kid given free reign in an ice-cream store. I am at peace, Father. And not alone. . . .

Father, it was through your efforts that I finally was able to receive a visit from the prison's chaplain last Thursday, and he said he'd visit me again and next time bring me Holy Communion! Thank you, thank you, with all my heart! Dear Father Connors has been great. He had contacted this priest before, but evidently the Catholic chaplain didn't understand that I didn't have any other priest bringing me the sacraments, and after your additional request, Father Connors looked into the matter again and renewed his request to the chaplain, who promptly responded. I was able to go to Confession. . . .

I do not know how much longer I will be here as I have been assigned to be transferred to Broward, a prison in south Florida, near Ft. Lauderdale. I feel fine about the transfer. I'm doing much better in my prayer life here than at Escambia County Jail, because of the solitary confinement and no TV blasting all day and most of the night. So I feel much better here than I did there, and Broward will be much like here because I'll still be in confinement. It's kind of like being on a retreat!! . . .

God bless you and keep you, dearest Father Tom. You are always in my heart and in my prayers. May the Mother of God hold you in her tender care. With love in Christ and Mary.

To Earl and Kathleen Essex: 9 November 1986, Lowell

Please don't worry about me. If I sounded tired, it was probably that I was a little concerned you and Tommy would, out of love for me, call the local priest here, Fr. Joe Connors, a very good priest and good man, and have him put pressure on the priest who has Mass at the prison in order to see me more often. And the reason I didn't want you to do that was simply because the priest told me he'd see me again soon and that he'd bring Holy Communion, and I believe he meant it. Just because he missed this last week doesn't mean he won't be coming this week. And the only reason he hasn't been coming to see me before his visit the week before last was because of a misunderstanding: he believed I had been seeing a priest regularly. . . . Anyway I just wanted to explain why my voice maybe didn't sound normal.

Believe me, dearest Earl, I am just fine. And I'm looking forward to Broward, too, if for no other reason than the fact that I'll be able to write with a pen again! I hate writing with a pencil. One of the inmates here in Confinement who did some time at Broward said that inmates in Confinement there were permitted to use pens. I can't wait to get there. Never thought something so little would mean so much. . . . Kathleen and Earl, I love you both. You are always in my prayers and held tenderly in my heart. God bless you. Mary hold you in her love.

Reflection on Non-cooperation upon Entering Broward Correctional: November 1986

There is the position that many direct action people espouse in support of cooperation while in jail because to them this means accepting injustice for the sake of Christ, gladly. My only variance, though I agree in principle with this, would be to say that I believe both approaches to be moral and justifiable depending upon the separate calling of the individual prolifer under conviction. Both cooperation with one's jail sentence and noncooperation . . . I believe to be meritorious . . . as long as the spiritual elements of courtesy, respect, kindness and humility are clearly present and reflected in either course of action. Motivation being, namely, that one believes the action to be pleasing to God and that in either action one conduct oneself as a Christian, with love, courteously, and regretfully for any hardship incurred by anyone (though that hardship may be necessary to cause a focus upon the truth), and in humility. This can, and indeed, need be one's disposition. Not defiant, but simply faithful to the dictates of one's heart and conscience.

Secondly, we must see a . . . distinction between the idea of a stance taken as witness that rejects cooperation with a system of evil—for example the court sentencing prolifers to punish them for rescuing babies, and to discourage others from doing likewise . . .and the spiritual, inner attitude and demeanor of the sentenced rescuer who does thank God joyfully for the privilege to suffer in His name and endure injustice for the sake of the more greviously offended preborn. By our love and humility and gentleness this attitude of accepting injustice upon oneself for Christ will shine through to others even while we non-cooperate in prison. We "non-cooperate" in love. In this way, for purposes of witness, of example, of purification, and thereby far from taking an easier road, we join ourselves more closely to the preborn who are abandoned by society.

Besides, we are not saying that we are better than other inmates and want to be treated better or differently. We are simply saying, yes, we are an inmate for Christ, but in conscience at this point and out of love for the babies and commitment to them we cannot cooperate with a sentence which is no insult to us, but rather is part of the structure of the holocaust. Part of its foundation. It is part of the compilation of actions and apathy without which the holocaust could not endure. The sentence attacks the humanity of preborn children everywhere and it attempts to halt rescue work by discouraging the rescue of these children. It is this with which we do not cooperate.

Actually, rather than being treated as though we're better than other inmates, we will be treated worse. We'll be put with the worst offenders, those who refuse to get along, with the loud and disruptive, with all the "worst" in the prison—those who continue to offend, who incur new charges, who refuse to cope, those who continue in hostility, who keep incurring trouble within prison itself; the saddest of the sad, the worst of the worst. And why should we not be with these?. . . . We will be cheerful, kind, and courteous, polite and humble with "our handlers," the officers over us; and helpful and kind with our fellow inmates. . . .

By our actions we'll set an example for those in the prison, those in the court, those in the community, and those in the prolife movement, which says that it is just not right to go along with injustice to the innocent preborn victims even in a small way, because even this small way, it too, contributes to the structure . . . that allows the holocaust to exist. It is no different than refusing to pay a fine to the court because that would be accepting the idea that you should be penalized for saving babies.

Of course, we do not non-cooperate to get a longer sentence or to suffer more: suffering will come as God allows and when we cannot avoid persecution. No, we say it is an attack on the dignity of preborn humanity to put rescuers in jail at all, whereby they cannot rescue more babies. However, if as a result of greater faithfulness . . . a longer sentence is incurred, a commitment to a worthy course of action presupposes a willingness to take the consequences. . . .

God gave us an intellect and I think he expects us to use it for the good. Strategy is simply the use of that intellect to best effect good by trying best to stop a terrible moral and physical outrage which horribly offends the Heart of God. We do not use strategy to take control from God, but to work with God's Will, His calling, His graces, His approved actions, to best touch the hearts of others and also to best prevent crimes against the natural law of God, the breaking of His Commandments. Certain sins we, as a community, have no control over. Others, however, such as legalized murder, we do have much control over, and we are duty bound to exert it. And I think God expects us to take this control, under His authority, as His instruments. Besides, God still has ultimate control. We acknowledge it and desire it. Thus we undertake certain actions, even if we were to know they would not be successful, simply due to faithfulness. . . .

Prayer indeed is of primary importance, but do not forget that part of prayer is prayer of action. Do not forget about both spiritual and corporal works of mercy, both of which are at work in a particular and fundamental way during a rescue mission. At all times, God is still in control as long as we acknowledge His control, desire His control, and ask for His control. . . . If our actions of strategy are aimed first at doing God's will, pleasing Him by using our mind to effect good—that is why we picket abortionists' homes, or judges' homes, to encourage them to extricate themselves from personal involvement and support of the holocaust—and if we act in every manner of love for all men, and sorrow for sin, our own and that of others, ultimately not being as concerned with results as with faithfulness to God, I believe God is pleased.

And though our first concern must be faithfulness to God's Holy Will, faithfulness to holiness, from which everything else flows, I believe God means us to be wise and use our minds to try to accomplish His good. . . . The two are meant to co-exist and to serve the same end: honor and glory to God. The triumph of good over evil. The accomplishment and fulfillment of His will.

Therefore, anything which denies God, attacks His truth or betrays it, can never be His means for ending the abortion holocaust. Thus, to stop abortion more effectively (supposedly) does not mean we are allowed to compromise another truth, as we have seen done by a faction in our movement that refuses to oppose artificial birth control. I am specifying those Catholics who know this to be evil. . . . Yes, some prolifers in willfully focusing on success in the abortion struggle have abandoned other moral truths, forgetting that truth, integrity, morality, in essence faithfulness, comes first and that success is not in our hands, but in God's. There is no contradiction here in conducting our efforts intelligently and with hope of success—as well as, and foremost, morally and faithfully. We are not permitted to sin in order to stop the holocaust. We cannot abandon God in order to accomplish our end.

If He has our hearts and our wills, He will lead us, be assured. . . . [W]ere it the witness He wants, we would do it even if it fails to be successful. In like manner, if we by our reason judge a certain action has no practical merit, we could discern that God would be better pleased if we use our minds to find a better way. And yet, we may also discern that He wants us to do it the ineffective way despite that fact, just as a matter of witness. That is why I think people are often called to different avenues of action because God wants us making many different witnesses.

Still. . . . I also believe God is so thoroughly outraged by the evil being supported by so many lukewarm, indifferent people of the "believing community," without whose support in a thousand little ways the evil could not exist, that I think He asks his activists to set an example of total and complete non-cooperation with any part of the structure, the process, which enables and supports the evil. And so we refuse to become a contributor in even the most minor and removed way. . . . I believe He wants His people to step further out into the waters and trust Him, even though we be misunderstood, perhaps. In time God will reveal the truth of our actions to those who truly have open hearts.

God also challenges us to think more deeply and pray more deeply through the beautiful help from brothers and sisters in the rescue movement, through the Church, the family, and others as well. My dear sister and fellow rescuer in St. Louis, Laura Dunn, has exerted this kind of beautiful influence on me, along with John Cavanaugh O'Keefe, John Ryan, Tom Herlihy, Joe Wall, my familial sisters Susan and Miriam, and others. I thank God for these magnificent people. They may not agree with my ideas or my actions every time, but they never fail to support me in their trust of me. And their challenging views never fail to touch me deeply and help to mold my opinions in so many ways. Spiritually, our gentle and humble mentor, Fr. Tom Cusack, has most clearly helped to lead me.

I ask those who have difficulty accepting this view on non-cooperation to think on and seriously contemplate the challenge to us of Franz Jaegerstaetter, who could have agreed to be a medic, perhaps in civil corps. . . . God bless you all.—Joan Andrews

[Franz Jaegerstaetter was an Austrian father and farmer who opposed the annexation of Austria by the Hitler regime in 1938, and refused conscription into the German military service in February 1943 on the grounds that, from a Catholic as well as natural perspective, the German war effort was both unjust and antiChristian. As a consequence of this position he was beheaded on 9 August 1943. Like Joan, Franz Jaegerstaetter also incurred opposition from his local bishops.]

5

Lead editorial in News/Sun Sentinel:
29 November 1986, Fort Lauderdale, Florida
Gene Cryer, editor; Kingsley Guy, editorial page editor

Thousands of supporters of jailed anti-abortion activist Joan Elizabeth Andrews have been jamming radio talk-show phonelines, bombarding prison officials and Gov. Bob Graham with calls and letters and planning huge protest rallies in an effort to get her a pardon.

Their cause is unjust. Andrews is unworthy of their support, and their pleas should be ignored. Andrews, a Broward Correctional inmate, should not be shown any leniency. She has repeatedly shown, both in and out of jail, that she is unwilling to abide by society's rules or cooperate with lawful authority, is unrepentant and will probably go on breaking the law if she is freed.... Pensacola judges rightly continue to deal harshly with pro-lifers like her who turn to illegal acts to protest abortions....

During commission of her crime, after her arrest and even after her trial, Andrews made it clear that she was on a crusade to protect unborn children, and that matters like people's private property and privacy rights and the law weren't about to get in her way. Originally sentenced to the medium-minimim [sic] security Florida Correctional Institution at Lowell, Andrews refused to follow orders or cooperate with prison officials, saying that to do so would be an admission of guilt. Because of that, she was sent to [Broward], a close-custody prison. There, she refused to be fingerprinted or complete her processing, so she has been placed in solitary confinement.

With good behavior, Andrews could become eligible for a work-release program after serving only 18 months, and be totally free after 2 1/2 years. But her refusal to follow lawful orders means that she will not be earning "gain time," and may end up serving the entire five years. Andrews may regard herself as some kind of martyr to a holy cause, but in reality she is just another of society's misfits who hasn't learned to respect other people's rights or to abide by the law.... Gov. Graham and Gov.-elect Bob Martinez should resist the pressure for leniency and let Andrews serve her full term in jail.

Lead Editorial, News/Sun Sentinel, Fort Lauderdale
2 December 1986
Gene Cryer, editor; Kingsley Guy, editorial page editor
Roswell Gilbert says he killed his wife Emily in an act of mercy. Now he is seeking mercy for himself. He deserves it. Gov. Bob Graham and Florida's six state Cabinet members should grant Gilbert executive clemency Thursday.

Report in the News Journal, Wilmington, Delaware:
27 November 1986
The assistant state's attorney in Pensacola called Joan Andrews a terrorist. The Catholic bishop in the area, Bishop J. Keith Symons, has said he cannot support her.

Report in the Tennesseean:
1 December 1986, Lewisburg, Tennessee

For years, Elizabeth Andrews had been struggling to understand why her daughters would go so far as to go to jail for their antiabortion views. Their cause became clearer this weekend when the 68-year-old Lewisburg woman herself was arrested for the first time in Pensacola, Fla., during protests over the imprisonment of her activist daughter Joan. . . . Andrews was among eight protesters arrested Friday when they blocked a car from driving to the Ladies Center, a clinic where abortions are performed. Eight others were arrested Saturday when they blocked the driveway of a judge who sentenced Andrews' daughter. It was a part of a weekend that attracted hundreds of abortion opponents from across the country. . . .

Report in The Marshall Gazette:
2 December 1986, Marshall, Tennessee

After Mrs. Andrews was placed in a patrol car, other members of the rally and prayer vigil knelt in front of the vehicle to prevent it from leaving. Mrs. Andrews asked them to let the car proceed saying, "This is an honor". . . . The Andrews are devout Roman Catholics and are a highly respected family in Lewisburg where they have lived for many years.

Editorial in Pensacola News Journal: 30 November 1986

Saturday's violent confrontation between police and pro-life protestors is an especially frightening development not because of what happened but because of what did not happen. As the level of violence and contempt for law in these pro-life marches escalates the chances of someone getting seriously injured or even killed greatly increases. . . . That's exactly what is going to happen if these so-called pro-life marches continue to be led by professional, out-of-town protestors whose singular [sic] goal is to precipitate violent confrontations, attract publicity and generate a never-ending list of jailed martyrs. . . .

Moreover, these out-of-town troublemakers not only showed their utter contempt for law and order, but chose to focus their hatred on a member of our judiciary, Judge William Anderson, who was doing his sworn duty and carrying out the laws of this state when he sentenced pro-life protester Joan Andrews to five years in prison for burglarizing the Ladies Center clinic in March. . . .

This is a city of enlightened, tolerant, peace-loving people, who respect law and order as well as the right to peacefully protest. But when professional rabblerousers and demogogues deliberately besmirch this city's good name and show their callous contempt for its laws, its police officers and its judiciary, then the time has come to enforce the law to its fullest and punish those who deserve punishment. . . . Still, it's tragic that such a fine city with so many God-fearing, patriotic citizens must suffer these tawdry protests by outside agitators whose true goals are highly questionable. But if that is to be our fate, then we must endure, show restraint and trust that our laws and system of justice will in the end prevail and see us through.

[On 4 December this paper published 54 letters relating to its editorial. Of the letters it chose to publish, 43 supported the paper's view, 3 were ambivalent, and 8 opposed it.]

Report in Pensacola News Journal: 3 December 1986

The president of the Pensacola Pro-Life Coalition Tuesday disavowed any association with out-of-town abortion protestors who came to Pensacola over the Thanksgiving holidays. The Rev. David Shofner said the coalition will meet Thursday with hopes of preparing a public statement disavowing criminal activity, rejecting unacceptable anti-abortion tactics, and perhaps apologizing to the City of Pensacola and a circuit court judge who was a protest target. . . .

Shofner . . . pastor of West Pensacola Baptist Church . . . said Anderson, who sentenced Andrews to prison only after she vowed to continue disobeying the law, is taking unfair criticism. "Judge Anderson did everything he could to keep her out of jail, and she just refused. . . . If Joan Andrews wants to be a martyr, she can be one, but my sympathy is not with Joan Andrews."

Resolution of Florida Right to Life: 28 March 1987
It is the policy of Florida Right to Life, Inc. not to engage in direct action of any kind, including such activities as picketing and sidewalk counseling specifically directed against abortion providers or their places of business. However, Florida Right to Life, Inc. recognizes and supports the rights of individuals to engage in lawful and non-violent direct action.

Report from National Catholic News Service: January 1987
Some pro-life leaders here are condemning demonstrations and actions organized by other abortion opponents to protest the jailing of an activist convicted of burglarizing an abortion clinic. . . . [S]uch actions have resulted in an "unfavorable climate," Sister Rose Vattilana, Pensacola-Tallahassee diocesan pro-life director, said in a written statement. She said an annual "Choose Life" walk for youth was cancelled because of it.

Editorial in Pensacola News Journal: 7 December 1986
Paul Jasper, editorial page editor
Today's . . . anti-abortionists . . . are not arrested for peacefully marching in the streets. They are arrested when they commit crimes. The crimes they commit are no technical violations designed to challenge the law: they are crimes

against people and property. When they are arrested, they are subdued with no more force than is absolutely necessary. When they are jailed, their rights are respected. And when they are sentenced, they are treated with just as much leniency as they deserve. . . . To trespass on the private property of Circuit Court Judge William Anderson who reluctantly sentenced one of the protesters to five years in prison after she refused to even promise to halt her illegal activities, is a travesty. . . . They ought to take out every fanatic in the world and shoot him down like a dog.

Memorandum of the Florida Catholic Conference:
10 December 1986
From executive director Tom Horkan, Jr. to all Florida bishops

I have received various telephone calls concerning Miss Andrews, and understand that various dioceses, diocesan offices, newspapers, pro-life and right to life offices have also received such calls concerning Ms. Andrews, with some rather grievous accusations against the court system and the prison system in Florida. I thought you would be interested in the following information. Miss Andrews was convicted of breaking into an abortion clinic in Pensacola, doing some damage and injuring some people [sic]. . . . At sentencing, all of the other defendants were permitted to go free on the basis of their assurance that they would not further break the law or approach the abortion clinic. Miss Andrews rejected probation on religious grounds and insisted that she was compelled to try to stop the killing of unborn children. . . . As a consequence the court sentenced her to five years in prison.

Miss Andrews is a conscientious objector to various things, including prison routine, and refused to take part in the orientation or other prison procedures for new prisoners at the women's prison at Lowell. . . . She was sent to a maximum security prison for women in Broward County, where

she also refused to submit to any of the orientation procedures, and adopted a passive resistance posture. Among
other things, I am told that she refused to go where she was
told to go, sat down and simply refused to move. She was
then placed in disciplinary confinement, which limits her visits to her attorney or religious visits. I am advised that the
Catholic chaplain at that prison has visited her weekly. She is
due to come out of restricted confinement today, but has advised the superintendent . . . that she will continue to refuse
to comply with the rules of the prison. If she does continue
to refuse, she will then be sent back to disciplinary confinement. She is being handled in the same way as any other
prisoner who refused to comply with the rules of the
prison. . . . Other than passive resistance, she is a cooperative
prisoner. . . .

I have reviewed portions of the court record, some materials being distributed on behalf of Miss Andrews, and
various news articles; and have spoken to various diocesan
officials, including [Pensacola] Bishop Symons; and also to
Wilson Bell of the Department of Corrections, and several
right to life people. . . . [I]t appears to me that the actions of
the court and the prison system are appropriate and in fact,
compelled by the actions of Miss Andrews. She has the key
to her maximum security cell. . . .

[Susan Brindle and Joan's family were upset by this
memo, in particular with the falsehood that Joan was convicted of injuring people. Attempts to have it amended were
met with hostilty and explicit lies from Horkan—see Memo
below—according to Susan Brindle. As a consequence, in
December 1986 the Andrews family wrote a letter to each of
the Florida bishops, which, in addition to correcting the er-
rors of the Catholic Conference memo, said also the following:]

Because she has not broken any of God's commandments or any moral law of this land . . . what ought our response to Joan's situation be? What does the Church teach? St. Thomas Aquinas [teaches]: "Human law has the nature of law in so far as it partakes of right reason; and it is clear that, in this respect, it is derived from the eternal law. But in so far as it deviates from reason, it is called an unjust law, and has the nature not of law but of violence." S.T., II.I, Q. 93, A. 3 ad 2. . . .

We hope and pray, your Excellency, that your response will be the morally rather than the socially acceptable one.

Second memorandum of Tom Horkan to Florida's Bishops: 17 February 1987

I forwarded to you a memorandum dated December 10, 1986 on [Joan Andrews]. It contained a sentence stating: "Miss Andrews was convicted of breaking into an abortion clinic in Pensacola, doing some damage and injuring some people." That sentence is somewhat inaccurate and should have read: "Miss Andrews was convicted of burglary of an abortion clinic in Pensacola and of resisting arrest." Burglary is defined in Florida law as "entering or remaining in a structure . . . with the intent to commit an offense therein. . . ."

A copy of the original found its way into the possession of Susan Andrews Brindle, the sister of Miss Andrews, who feels that it is not only false, but seriously offensive and maligns her sister. Thus the corrective memorandum.

[The ellipses above are Mr. Horkan's and also instructive. They delete the qualifying information about Florida's burglary law which adds: "unless the premises is at the time open to the public."]

From the Office of Edward McCarthy, Archbishop of Miami to Miriam McCue: 28 August 1987

Archbishop McCarthy received your letter in reference

to Joan Andrews ... [P]lease be assured that the Bishops of the Province of Florida continue to advocate on Joan's behalf. ... In Christ, The Reverend Pablo A. Navarro, Secretary to the Archbishop of Miami

From Fr. Paul Quay to Joan Andrews: 13 December 1986
I called Warden Villacorta a few days back, and was glad to learn from her that you can receive our Lord in Communion each week and have the opportunity for Confession as well. She also said that if Fr. Santos was willing, he could say Mass in the space outside your cell so you could in that way be present. ...

[Despite said permission, the Archdiocese of Miami refused to provide a Mass for Miss Andrews throughout 1987. A Constitutional question was raised, however, by Broward's refusal to let Andrews attend the regular weekly Mass held there.]

From The American Life League (Richard Cowden Guido)
to Governor Martinez's Staff: 27 December 1987
The American Life League's national director, Judie Brown, held extensive conversations with Vatican officials in Rome about the Andrews case in October [Brown was in Rome in connection with the Synod on the Laity which was being held at that time]. They asked for a full report, which task she assigned to me, and that report will soon be ready. Of particular concern to the Vatican was Ms. Andrews's access to the Catholic Sacraments, and I am happy to report the kind cooperation of Broward warden Marta Villacorta—both with me, and in insuring that Ms. Andrews has had ready access (given the circumstances) to both the Sacraments of Confession and Holy Communion.
Prison rules by which Ms. Villacorta feels bound, however, have denied Ms. Andrews access to any Holy Mass for

over seventeen months, though Catholics are bound in conscience on pain of serious sin at least to attend Mass weekly, and sometimes more than weekly, as for example on Christmas. This is a complicated matter, due from the Correctional perspective to Ms. Andrews's political position of (to be sure, friendly) non-cooperation. As a consequence, Ms. Andrews has been in solitary confinement for these seventeen months. Nonetheless, there is a serious Constitutional question that arises here, which I have discussed with, among others, First Amendment expert Nat Hentoff . . . who has of course been following the case.

Since Joan Andrews is no physical threat to the order of prison routine, the Constitutional question is whether the State has the legal right to deny her attendance at the Holy Mass which is held weekly at Broward, as a condition of her solitary confinement. During the Judiciary Committee hearings on the Supreme Court nomination of Anthony Kennedy, the issue of privacy was crucial—Robert Bork's perspectives on these matters can even be said to have defeated his nomination.

What Judge Kennedy said is that American law, tradition, that the American people, recognize "a zone of privacy" past which the State has no right to go. Leaving aside the more general questions of justice in the Andrews case: must a Roman Catholic who engages in the same kind of civil disobedience for which Dr. Martin Luther King Jr. (who was lauded by Pope John-Paul II in New Orleans last September) is recognized as a national hero, have to sacrifice her right to attend Christmas Mass as a consequence? Or does this violate that zone of Ms. Andrews's privacy, which it is not the province of the State to violate? . . .

Letter from Florida Department of Corrections (Harry K. Singletary, Jr., Assistant Secretary for Operations)
to Miriam McCue: 15 June 1987

I have received your letter ... regarding inmate Joan Andrews, #151909. You wrote to request that she be allowed to attend religious services, specifically the Mass, despite her status in disciplinary confinement. ... My knowledge of Catholicism is not as extensive as yours, but I believe the Church stipulates that Mass is only required of those who are capable of attending. Those who cannot attend are provided exceptions and do not commit a sin when they are unable to go to Mass. Therefore, inmate Andrews is not in a state of sin because we will not allow her to participate in the Mass. ...

Until inmate Andrews is processed, she will continue to receive disciplinary action and this will prohibit her involvement in any programs available at the institution. ...

Memorandum from Richard Cowden Guido to Judie Brown:
25 January 1988

It should be remembered that Andrews has been denied a Mass for over a year and a half now, not because of the alleged crime for which she was convicted, but solely as a result of her political position of non-cooperation. Nat Hentoff frankly calls this illegal, since a Mass was held each week at Broward; in his view, the State violates her First Amendment privileges by virtue of nothing more than an administrative ruling.

The matter is further complicated, however, as a result of much hostility to Andrews on the part of the Diocese of Pensacola, the Archdiocese of Miami, and the Florida Catholic Conference. There has been at least a de facto collusion between the Church and State on this matter, and though there is no direct evidence of a formal collusion, the situation as of today would be no different had there been.

Joan's treatment by the State has been publicly defended by Pensacola Bishop Kieth Symons; and in a formal memorandum sent to all of Florida's bishops by the Florida Catholic Conference executive director Thomas Horkan. Despite claims to having read through the trial transcripts, Horkan told the Florida episcopate that Joan had been convicted of "injuring people," which was not true: neither had she injured anyone, nor been convicted of such. Further, according to Andrews's sister Susan Brindle, when confronted about this rather serious misstatement, Horkan denied having issued it. She also claims that Horkan became hostile and abusive to her by phone, when later confronted with this explicit falsehood. In January 1988 Horkan confirmed the difficult nature of the second phone conversation to me, but denied that their dispute had anything to do with the misstatement about injuring people—a rather strange denial in that he had on 17 February 1987 already issued a somewhat cold corrective memo on precisely that point (the original memo was on 10 December 1986).

Meanwhile, though the State refused to allow Andrews access to the regular Mass at Broward, and though it would not allow any outside priest into the prison to say Mass for her, it did agree, at least by December 1986, to allow the formal Miami Archdiocesan prison chaplain, Father Mark Santos, to say a Mass by and/or in her cell. Because of time and other pressures, this would have been difficult to do on a regular basis—but it was not done once, not for Easter or Christmas or on any other occasion, throughout 1987, and no attempt was made by Miami Archbishop Edward McCarthy, Father Santos, the Florida Catholic Conference, or any employee of the Church in Florida to give her this pastoral assistance.

I called Father Santos and asked him why. He was very hostile, and frankly stated that "if she wanted to hear a Mass, she should have cooperated." I called the Archdiocese of Miami and explicitly asked if the reason it made no effort to provide Andrews a Mass was its conviction that this was an appropriate means to force her off her position of non-cooperation, which it clearly did not support. The Archdiocese refused to comment. I asked why it refused throughout 1987 to provide her with the Mass the State would have allowed in her cell, despite public claims by Archbishop McCarthy's personal Secretary that "the Bishops of the Province of Florida continue to advocate on Joan's behalf." Again, the Archdiocese refused to comment. When I spoke to Thomas Horkan, I asked if the Florida Catholic Conference had done anything on Ms. Andrews's behalf either to ensure her access to the weekly Mass at Broward, or to see that she could hear the Mass the State would allow. The answer to both questions was negative. When I asked why, he said, "I haven't thought that much about it." When I asked if the Florida Catholic Conference intended to do anything in the future on this matter, he clearly indicated he thought it would be a waste of time.

The main reason it seems unlikely there was any formal collusion between Church and State on this matter, is simply that such collusion was not necessary: the Church knew the position of the State; formally supported it through the Florida State Catholic Conference in the 10 December memorandum by Horkan as well as by public statements from Pensacola Bishop Keith Symons and his diocesen pro-life director Sister Rose Vattilana; and effectively supported it in the field through Father Santos at Broward, and the chaplain at Escambia, who, as Joan points out in the enclosed letter, considers pro-lifers to be "pretty despicable."

As you know, this picture began to change last December regarding some episcopal involvement in the Andrews case, in particular New York Archdiocesan auxiliary Bishop Austin Vaughan's public assertion at the Catholics United for the Faith dinner that Joan Andrews is entitled "to the

collective support of us all." Nonetheless, all formal episcopal support at this time has focused on her support for rescue, and her witness for the unborn. That is as she would
want it, but my point is that it has still been eighteen months
since this remarkable Catholic woman has illegally been denied her right to attend Mass—and that no priest I know of
(many have unsuccessfully tried to get in to see her) has
publicly challenged this crime: no Florida Catholic cleric has
yet even interceded to try and put a stop to it—and this latter, due not a little to the bishops' (or anyhow their appa-
rats) political, not religious, opposition to her position on
non-cooperation.

To put the matter in focus: Because Joan Andrews on
Catholic moral law grounds refuses to recognise either the
legitimacy of legal abortion, or the right of the State to pe-
nalize those who seek to stop the immediate planned killings
at an abortion center—because of that opinion, remember,
and not because of the alleged crime for which she was convicted—the State has retaliated by denying her the right to
hear a Catholic Mass. This position has the formal and practical support of Miami Archbishop Edward McCarthy, and
the Florida Catholic Conference.

Lay pressure on this matter, in particular the American
Life League's on both the political and legal fronts, is wide,
and ought to secure a Mass for Miss Andrews shortly. Private or public support from the Vatican could not hurt in
helping to see the attainment of that goal. Since Cardinal
Ratzinger will be in New York on Wednesday I will try to
pass this to him then. In any event, this is the information the
Curial Cardinals requested.

6

From Joe Wall to Richard Cowden Guido: 15 November 1986

A couple of days ago, Joan was moved to Broward Correctional Institute, Florida's maximum security facility. When Susan learned of this, she called the Warden there and [apprised] her of Joan's background. The Warden responded, "What is she doing in a place like this, this is for violent prisoners? If they [the other inmates] learn she is peaceful, they will gang up on her." [It was also at this point that Andrews was subjected to that threat by the R&O lieutenant—presumably without Villacorta's knowledge—as described in the introduction of this book.] A reasonable hypothesis would be that her non-violent non-cooperation while in prison has made them resolve to break her, and so they have sent her to this "Devil's Island" of Florida for special treatment.

Poor little Joan. She is undergoing this torment alone, save for Christ by her side. She has been deserted by all but a few faithful friends like John Ryan, her two sisters, and a few others. The American Life League has stood by her, and *The Wanderer* to some extent, but most national pro-life groups have ignored her. And Bishop Symons of Pensacola says, "I support the judiciary," reminding one of his brother bishops in another era, who supported the persecution of yet another Joan.

From Joan Andrews to Jessica Shaver:
Undated, Broward Correctional

Broward is Florida's only maximum security women's prison. There are over 500 inmates here. All except those (roughly 50) of us here in the confinement unit and the death row unit, live out on the compound in dormitory buildings. They are allowed privileges such as telephone use, commissary use, visitors, recreational facilities, jobs, prison movies, television in the dorms, and can somewhat freely walk about the premises as long as they carry a pass.

I cannot use the telephone nor receive visitors, not even immediate family. This is part of the punishment. Along with this, gain-time is taken (or never earned), which means I will not get an early release.... All this is a high price to pay for principle—for my decision to non-cooperate. I realize this. And yet I firmly believe in what I am doing....

No government can operate without the support of the populace. All it takes is a very small, but visible and deter-mined, minority willing to suffer and even die for truth and justice in order to force a change in judicial, governmental, or social policy.... [A] nation cannot stand under the weight of a holocaust if there's a strong enough outcry against it. Prolifers must be willing to suffer and to act, or else be will-ing to live through many more decades of slaughter....

I am sitting on my bunk writing. The din of noise in the confinement unit is very loud, as usual. It reverberates through the concrete and steel walls, and does, in fact, con-jure up an image of a modern day dungeon. My heavy steel door has a narrow slat in it, with mesh iron, and I am able with some difficulty to look out at the two tiers of cells, up-per and lower, the iron railings, narrow walkway, and the bars at the entrance to the unit. . . . There is one window in my cell, but it is painted over so that an inmate cannot see out and no light comes in. It is also screened off by a heavy iron mesh. There is much graffiti on the walls, mostly obscene, but I have been able to blacken out most of the worst. The floor is concrete. . . .

The warden at Broward is a good woman, and I believe she is a Christian. I have the utmost respect for her. Marta Villacorta is not only a fair person, caring and decent, but she has the interest of the inmates at heart as well as the interests of the correctional staff and the prison itself. This prison is blessed to have her. I do not support everything she authorizes, and I'm sure she doesn't support my position, nor some of my views, but I respect her sincerity.

With me in my cell I have my Bible, my breviary and my rosary. It is the greatest consolation and joy to study the Scriptures and to pray, giving thanks to God for His constant blessings and His care. I do not think I could make it without the rosary. Another inmate and I read Scripture to each other through our doors, and sometimes others join us.

It is beautiful to see how Our Dear Lord reaches out and touches hearts. I have been so deeply blessed by the officers and fellow inmates in here. There is certainly much tragedy, heartache, and brutality here, but there are also signs of goodness and love, and acts of caring. God is present, even here, just as He is present at the abortion death camps, particularly when we become His arms, His legs, and His voice, being there present ourselves to pray and to plead. . . .

Jessica, I guess the greatest pain of prison for me is being separated from my family and loved ones. Though I am not married and have no children, I am very close to my nephews and nieces and I miss them terribly. It is very lonely here. And yet of course there is always our Sweet Savior . . . and His mother as our gentle consolation. Tears may come, but in the end it always wells up in rejoicing. How can it not? . . . May the dear Lord hold you in His tender care always. Your sister in Jesus and Mary.

To Joe Wall: 28 October 1987, Broward Correctional

Whether I am DC (Disciplinary Confinement) or AC (Administrative Confinement) I am unable to receive any visitors. The only concrete and real difference between DC & AC is that while in DC I cannot have any press interviews, whereas in AC I can. However, I can see my attornies—Earl Essex, Tom Herlihy, Judge Johnson and Peter Lennox at any time as long as they prearrange their visit.

One new development as of September 1987 [sixteen months after the original imprisonment, ten after coming to Broward] is that on occasion Mrs. Villacorta will allow me to see my immediate family members. Theoretically, I can have canteen privileges on AC by filling out a canteen slip and drawing bank from my inmate account. However, the reality rarely takes place because it takes 7-10 days to complete the process and by the time I have completed it I am back in DC again and cannot get to the canteen. I am allowed personal property—clothes, radio, etc.—but since I have no personal property, this is of no value to me. I never move from my cell in confinement. The change is only on paper, not in reality. As soon as I turn AC I am ordered to participate and cooperate, which I refuse, and a DR (Disciplinary Report) is written on me—thus I stay confined, but under investigation (AC status) until my DR hearing. At the hearing I am always given the punishment of 30 days DC confinement and the loss of 60 days gain time. While AC I stay confined and get out of my cell for one hour each day during the week, though not on any weekends—the same as DC status . . . last week-end I took my first shower in three months! What a treat! I clean up alone of course, but stopped taking showers due to total lack of privacy.

The gal in the cell next to mine has learned about novenas [a novena is a period of nine days of prayer with particular petitions] today and we have agreed to go on a novena together starting tomorrow. We will abstain from all meat and pray together often during the days, including the Memorare. Pretty good for a nice Baptist girl! . . .

The dear and good priest Fr. Santos has not been able to say Mass for me yet, but he is trying very hard to work it out. The prison won't allow any other priest to come in to do it, and Fr. Santos must run between about three prisons. He is doing the best he can, and trying very hard to arrange to say a Mass for me, though I will not allow that if it means he would have to cancel for the other inmates at the other prisons. I am confident God will find a way for me to attend a Mass somehow. God bless you dearest Joe.

10 December 1986, Broward Correctional
Thank you for being my rescuer time and time again. Yes, Joe, I did receive your marvelous letter detailing my little Mama's arrest. I was so proud of her! And I was also most deeply touched by your fervor in sticking by her side all the way to the police car. . . . Thank God the abortionist never came, and that not a single baby was put to death in Pensacola while the prolife rescue workers were there! . . . I am so proud of you, Joe. What a hero you are to me! To all of us. . . .

17 November 1986
Tragically, most everyone in the prison population is homosexually active, and they carry on constantly about their inmate lover(s). Seems to be the standard way of life here, and pretty much at Lowell too. In fact, as I was telling Susan, most of the assaults and killings in both prisons occur over "lovers quarrels." Anyway, you can see life is pretty messed up here. It's the saddest of the sad, I think. Please keep these

poor souls (all of us) in your prayers.

I am still doing well. When I get cowardly or scared about something, I can feel everyone's prayers and God's grace just envelops me. And for some reason, (it has to be the tender compassionate Heart of our God), I find Him easing my fears and handling situations so that they turn out easier on me than I thought they'd be. Dear God is always so good to us. It makes me want to be better. We can never ever love Him as we should, but wouldn't it be heaven if we could. . . . Love.

From Elie Weisel's Nobel Speech: December 1986

Sometimes we must interfere. When human lives are endangered, when human dignity is in jeopardy . . . wherever men or women are persecued because of their race, religion, or political views, that place must—at that moment—become the center of the universe.

From Joan Andrews to Father Paul Quay, S.J.:
5 January 1987, Broward Correctional

The conditions here are rather prohibitive as I am in the confinement block of the prison due to my non-cooperative status. I am allowed to write letters, but practical matters (i.e. writing paper) makes this limited. Mail is searched—incoming and outgoing, as well as authorized to be read by prison personnel. . . . I can never have visitors, not even family, and I can never use the phone. The only exception to both rules is that I may have an attorney's visit, and I may call an attorney if the call is approved. So far in the seven weeks I've been at Broward, I have not had a phone call to my attorney approved. Red tape, I guess. It has caused some great problems to the point that I will advise my attorney via letter to cancel my appeal.

I have not been able to attend the Holy Mass, however a priest does come once a week for a few minutes to hear my

Confession and bring me the Most Blessed Sacrament. For this I am very grateful. Other priests have not been allowed to see me so far. One who came, a friend from Philadelphia, was told he could not see me since the Catholic priest attached to the prison has been seeing me. Father, I am most grateful for your efforts on my behalf to procure permission for me to have the Mass said on the walkway outside my cell. God love you! I pray this will be done sometime soon. The poor priest who has duties here is very overburdened and does not have much time. But I am sure he will try to do this sometime. Thank you for getting the permission for this. . . .

I firmly believe . . . we should physically make the community deal with us, put us out of the way, in order to carry out the killing in any given community. . . . This holocaust could not exist if even just the avowed prolifers in this country decided in unison to refuse all cooperation with it. It doesn't take large numbers, but it does take great dedication by the few. . . .

I thank you, Father, for your prayers and remembrance in the Mass. I do so appreciate prayers asking Our Dear Lord to help me to grow spiritually strong. I want to be holy, but the struggle is so difficult. . . .

The Jesuits, the one time great defenders of the Pope and the Faith, will surely regain their sanctity, their vigor, and the Truth in time. I hope, and pray, it will not be long in coming. . . . Dearest Father Quay, may God bless you and all your labors, your beloved Mother, and all those whom you hold dear, and may Mary, the Mother of Christ and our Mother, hold you close in her tender care. Yours in Christ and Mary.

To brother Bill and his wife, Claudia:
19 January 1987, Broward Correctional
Concerning my day to day existence in prison which you asked about, Bill, particularly with regard to how I cope with

the homosexual situation, I must admit it is difficult. However, I am no longer in population. I am now in solitary confinement, so that I am not physically exposed to it as I have been in the past. However, even now I hear the constant verbalization of this sad, tragic and dehumanizing condition in which the vast majority of the inmates degrade themselves. The only thing one can do in such a situation is to pray a great deal.

Before I was moved into solitary, all of my cellmates were homosexually active. They knew I was a practicing Christian and they left me alone; and when I tried talking with one of the women whom I had begun praying with often throughout the day and night, she immediately cut me off. She did not want to face the truth of her action. She knew. But just didn't want to give up her "lovers." Of course, such perversion breeds anger, hostility, frustration, hate, violence, and disease. Which can all be seen in a microcosm in prison, intensely magnified.

God is good. He gives us strength for prayer, patience, sacrifice, and forebearance in such situations. Therefore, keep me in your prayers, dear Bill and Claudia, but do be assured that I am coping as well as can be expected, and that I am at peace with my situation. . . .

The days are long and pass slowly, the nights sometimes longer; the greatest burden beyond the pain, hostility, and self-destruction one sees constantly, is the ache of being deprived of family and friends. Especially for me, as I ache to have children of my own, and time is very precious to me. And yet, what choice do I have while living amidst such a brutal holocaust, except to act out Christian love in the form of rescue attempts? Tragically, this puts us in prison, but then others certainly suffer much more: the preborn and newborn children dying, as well as those doing the killing and those supporting the killing, who are deforming their minds and their hearts, and most tragically of all, risking the loss of their immortal souls! God save them! These are the ones who suffer the most. . . .

May God bless you and keep you always, Bill and Claudia, and may Mary ever be at your side. Thank you for your prayers. I love you.

To Peter Lennox: 11 January 1987, Broward Correctional

I will probably allow my appeal to continue . . . because in my weakness, I do so desire to be released from this prison. I hope I am not going against Our Lord's will in this. . . . All my love in Christ and Mary.

15 January 1987, Broward Correctional

I'm afraid the devil has been attacking me bitterly in here these last two months. It seems that all I want to do every waking moment is pray—and yet my prayers are so weak and distracted. I am sure it is emotional and psychological exhaustion, not physical, but it is hard to deal with. I trust God totally of course. Who could not! And yet, I can't seem to serve Him and be at least somewhat holy—though I certainly want to be. The problem is that I've allowed myself to succumb to unguarded thoughts. There is so much obscenity abounding, and it is all I hear.

Please understand, I am not making excuses. At Lowell, the environment was just as oppressive, but I dwelled in God's grace and never knew such bliss and heavenly joy. I recall that when I was being transported to Broward, a fellow inmate, convicted of murder, said she would not live out one year in prison, she would take her own life first. I pleaded with her and talked to her of God, but she was so horrified at being in shackles and enduring life in prison that she could not bear the thought of even a few years of such. She only had an eight to ten year sentence, I think. With gain time, she'd be out in three or four. I told her all this. She kept stressing 'quality of life' and I told her surely she could bear a few hard years for the assured 'quality of life' in the future, a mere four years ahead. She didn't care. I told her regardless of anything else, if she took her life and should face hellfire—no torment, no sorrow, no existence was as painful as that—to lose Christ! To even chance it! Even if she were not a believer, didn't know if there was a God, how could she chance it? None of my arguments mattered to her. She said to me: "Prison changes you. You become an animal. I won't live that way!" Then she asked me, "How long have you been in?" I told her and she said, "Then you know. You've be n in as long as I have. It has changed you, hasn't it?"

Maybe I should have answered her directly. My unspoken answer was yes, it has changed me, but for the better! I am a better person now because of prison, through God's mercy and grace. It had changed me for the better, and it could do the same for her. This is what my answer was at that time. And it remains true as long as one accepts God's grace. However, because I've lost grips with living in God's grace, I am suffering the effects of prison in a dreadful way.

At that time, though, on November 13th, I did not tell this poor woman that rather than becoming less human, I felt I had become more fully human because of the Divine love of Christ, and through living this painful experience with Him. I at least told her she could find joy, peace, love, and ultimate total dignity and worth through Christ, whether in prison or anywhere. Maybe I should have made it personal. I just felt that my testimony of joy despite my surroundings might wound her in her misery. At one point in the journey, which took all day, she struggled against her handcuffs which held her hands close to her side by the waist chains. I feared she was going to lose control of herself and become violent and hysterical, but she finally fell into a listless stupor [and] just stared out as if unseeing. This poor soul. Certainly I was unable to reach her with God's love for her. She just closed herself off in her misery.

I think back now on our conversation which after awhile she had told me was bothering her, and she told me to say no more to her. Prayer was the only tool at that point. As poor as our prayers may be, God sees our hearts, and He understands. He understands now, too, despite the spiritual misery I am presently in, due to my sins. I long for the joy and the peace I had in my spiritual life up until late November. I certainly no longer hold as true the personal answer I would have given Pat to the question of hadn't jail changed me into a miserable creature. I am quite miserable in my sinfulness now.

I still know the truth. I know God forgives. And I am indeed sorry for my wretched sinfulness. But you know, Peter, it just hurts so to offend God, Who is all good and all holy. I don't want to sin against Him anymore. Only God is holy, but He gives us the grace to reflect His Holiness ... personally accepted, utterly cared for, and loved—unconditionally so. It's the way all Christians should really be with each other! That is how we will be in the reign of God.

Pray for my faithfulness to Him, that I may serve Him according to His will. He's here, but I can't find Him for my wretched sinfulness. Yet I know Our Dear Savior is here, calling to me. Help me by your prayers to see Him and answer Him. May God in His supreme goodness bless you, guard you, protect you, guide you, and smile upon you all the days of your life until you are joined eternally with Him in Heaven; and may the Mother of Jesus, Mary Queen of Angels, hold you in her tender care, always. Your sister in Christ, Our Lord.

24 January 1987, Broward Correctional

The noise was so deafening last night that a Lieutenant came in and informed us that if the noise did not cut down at once the whole confinement block would be put in strip cells. I had seen inmates put in strip cells before, usually for violence or acting out in a bad way. One's cell is stripped completely bare, all sheets, blankets, clothes, personal items—everything—is taken out. Even the toilet paper is taken away, as well as the mattress, and the inmate is stripped naked. In addition, if the inmate fights the process, by continued belligerence or violence, she is put in shackles, the extent of which depends upon her behavior. Last night, after the warning, the noise kept up unabated for a while, but then as several cells were being stripped, the majority lowered their voices, and it ended up where only four or five women were the ones to suffer the punishment threatened upon all of us. Because at least two of these women put up some resistance, they were put in shackles. Actually, only one got the full treatment—leg irons, waist chains and handcuffs down to the waist: the other was simply put in handcuffs. The sad thing is that one of the women—Yolanda [not her real name]—can't help herself much, the way she behaves. She never obeys orders. She sometimes raves all day and all night at the top of her lungs. She ended up in chains. . . .

Last night after lights out, I tried to get my prayers said. With most of my praying, I usually pace my cell. So for three and a half hours, I paced and tried to concentrate as poor Yolanda wailed. . . . About the time it quieted down, I finished my prayers and went to bed. I felt so comfortable in my covers and thought how miserably cold those in the strip cells must be lying naked on the concrete floor or the metal bunk. Yolanda had cried and pleaded about having tried to sleep sitting on the toilet, but even that was too cold a surface. Yolanda calls on Jesus very often and prays and gives "sermons," but when agitated, like last night, she is a different person. Yet, she never curses God or blames Him. She simply puts Him aside for awhile. . . . God bless you. In

Christ's love.

Undated, Broward Correctional
God love them! There can be cruelty, and behavior so crushingly self-destructive ... and yet they have hearts and exhibit caring and goodness too. In all my experiences in jails, I've never met a fellow inmate I didn't like. The spark of God's love in each one always found its way to the surface somehow. I am sure that is true of all people. ... I can't wait to hold Michael and Philip [the Lennox children] on my lap and, if it won't scare them, give them hugs and kisses, and al¹ those dreadful things little boys don't particularly like, least wise from strangers. ... Your sister in Christ and Mary

Lay Letter to Pope John Paul II: 14 January 1987
The enclosed, which appeared in the 1 January *Wanderer*, deserves your attention. Inasmuch as you are going to Florida this year, and Joan Andrews, about whom the enclosed article speaks, is clearly making an heroic, and arguably saintly, witness on behalf of the unborn, would you consider sending a personal note of encouragement to her? Or making a public statement on her behalf, both before and during your Florida trip (though, after prayers for her, I am sure she would prefer a private, personal note most of all)?

From Joan Andrews to her parents:
28 January 1987, Broward Correctional
Daddy, I enjoyed hearing that you and John were picking up hay together. I used to love those trips to get hay. Is John getting a percentage of the hay cut at Hillsboro farm, or did you just buy the hay in that area, Daddy, and store it at John's farm?
Mama, no silver rosary has arrived from you. Maybe it is just being delayed a while. I'll let you know as soon as it arrives. Do not worry, I will take good care of it and not give it

away. However, if it is returned to you, please do not resend it. I don't want to chance your losing it in the mail. Besides, I do have a couple rosaries ... which a St. Louis police officer sent me (he used to book me and the other pro-lifers when we were arrested in St. Louis County. He's great. Always slips me a rosary through the bars, or sends me one when he hears I'm in jail elsewhere). I love you. God Bless. Lights out.

To Peter Lennox: 5 February 1987, Broward Correctional

It's been raining outside all day, which means I won't be able to have my walk in the yard this evening; but that disappointment is counter-balanced by the joy it is to hear the rain against my window. Though I cannot see it since the window is painted out, I can picture a beautiful wet world. I love to be out in the rain.

Poor Yolanda Brency, about whom I wrote you once, keeps getting worse and worse. She rarely uses God's name in praise anymore in her almost singsong ravings; now she calls upon Jesus to do evil. Asking Him to kill people and harm them in a torturous manner. When we spoke on the phone, Peter, you mentioned that you had told Mrs. Villacorta that you knew people who would like to write and otherwise help other inmates as well. Could you ask some of these people to write Yolanda? I don't know her DC # but letters would reach her. And of course, if everyone could keep her in prayer.... God is powerful. Prayers and the show of love and concern could bring Yolanda out of her private hell.... Also maybe a card once in a while could be sent to Marsha Manning [not real names].... She has become dedicated to Jesus since her imprisonment.... Rachel has no family, no one cares about her or writes her ... she was a runaway when she was very young.... Teresa Parker has many family problems. She's trying to get her children back once she's released, which should be in a few months, and her house is threatened by foreclosure. . . .

Scarlett Anderson is pregnant. Could someone send her prolife literature and moral support? She wanted to abort the baby but her mother could not come up with the money, thank God! Through a very nice correctional officer, I've put her in touch with a prolife Christian ministry . . . she plans to give the baby up for adoption. . . . In His Love.

To Dana Lennox: 25 January 1987, Broward Correctional
Yesterday and today have been quite unbelievable. There is an inmate with whom I spend nearly all my time recently (we're both locked in separate cells but are in constant communication). It's Yolanda Brency whom I wrote you and Peter about once or twice. She has found some security in my friendship, for which I am grateful, but most of the time she is in need of the Lord and His Word, so I spend much time reading the Bible to her through the crack in my door. Being in a strip cell for the past three weeks, she does not have her Bible with her. The Bible which you and Peter gave me—my most cherished gift—is such a solace. I think of you and pray for you whenever I look upon it and read and meditate from it. How dear you are to me and forever will be. . . . Love.

To Michael and Philip Lennox:
5 March 1987, Broward Correctional
I've heard that you and the whole family have been sick for quite a while. This makes me sad. I pray that you will be all well very soon and that you will stay well always. It's not any fun being sick. But while we are sick and waiting for dear God to make us better, we can ask Jesus to take our suffering as a prayer for all those in the world who need their hearts and their souls to be made better. By not complaining while we are sick and being cheerful, maybe some poor person will be blessed by our prayer to Jesus and will come to

love Him as everyone should. He knows it is not easy to smile when we are hurting and feeling sick. He even understands when we can't smile and when we have to cry. Our dear God is so wonderful! He is so gentle with us. . . . God bless you my little angels.—Joanie

To Peter and Dana Lennox:
7 March 1987, Broward Correctional
Some days I spend much time talking with and reading the Bible with Yolanda Brency. I had put in a request about three weeks ago to allow us to be bunkies. I felt maybe I could be a good influence on her. It was worth a try. But I doubt that will ever happen now. She would either talk with me or curse me out depending on her quick-changing moods, and I've stayed her friend whenever she's been willing to accept me back into friendship. But two days ago she went off in a bad way and attacked three officers. Now that she has a new outside charge (assault on an officer) and will be going to court on it, all requests are being denied her. She was just about to get out of her strip cell too, she had gotten a blanket two days before, and had gotten her mattress the night before, and would have been able to get one piece of property back each day thereafter if she had remained well behaved. I had asked her to ask for her Bible. But she cursed out the lieutenant when the latter left her cell during the middle of the conversation to respond to an emergency in the cell next door (the inmate there was throwing a tantrum and threatening violence).

Yolanda became very angry and one thing led to another, and before long she had busted her light and was threatening to cut her throat if anyone touched her. They maced her and got the glass, and took everything from her cell. When they showered her later to get the mace off her, she attacked the three officers. Even the one small window in the door is all sealed up now because she was throwing waste on the officers. It is really tragic. For almost a week she was doing so well. She'd still go off, but was usually able to be talked into control, and gotten to behave again through reading the Bible to her and discussing the passages. Please keep her in prayer. It's the only thing that can help her. Like at the death camps, sometimes one can just feel the glee of the devil here. . . .

On Saturday mornings the Catholic priest usually comes to see me for about 15 minutes, and I receive the Sacraments!!! . . . God bless you!

Lead eitorial in the National Catholic Register: 8 March 1987

People shouldn't be sent to prison for trying to save lives. . . . Joan Andrews has been saving lives for a long time. . . . She's a woman of gentleness and courage.

There's a common-law doctrine that recognizes a legal defense based on "necessity" or "justification," meaning that one is justified in breaking a law to achieve a greater good. The classic case is trespassing on property in order to save a child in a burning building. In such a case, the trespassers commit no crime; they are considered heroes and may, indeed, be given medals.

Prolifers who engage in sit-ins or rescue missions are not looking for medals. But they believe they should be allowed the defense of necessity. We agree. Judges should allow juries to hear this defense. When they do not, or when they instruct jurors to disregard this defense, it's well to recall John Adams's 1771 essay on the rights of juries. Speaking of the juror faced with faulty instructions from the bench, Adams said: "It is not only his right but his duty in that case to find the verdict according to his own best understanding, judgment and conscience, though in direct opposition to the direction of the court."

When the defense of necessity has been ignored at a lower court level (as in the Andrews case, which involved a non-jury trial), an appeals court can correct the situation. We hope the appeals court in Florida will do so. If it does not, we urge Gov. Robert Martinez and his cabinet to use their power of clemency and remedy the injustice done to Joan Andrews.

From Joan Andrews to Jeff Frye:
18 February 1987, Broward Correctional

Jeff, I am very glad you are not quitting the National Federation of the Blind, despite the upsetting defeats of your prolife resolutions. They need you, Jeff . . . though I am glad they know their true blindness, their moral blindness, upset you enough to provoke the possibility of resignation. . . . I would really love to attend one of the state or national conventions with you sometime, Jeff. Do you think maybe I could? . . .

To back up just a moment, I'd like to say one other thing about your comments concerning faith and works. Jeff, I love your perception in this. We're saved . . . by faith. But how can we love God as He is reflected in each of us if we act not Godly? Christians are supposed to "put on the Lord Jesus Christ" and behave as such. Christians must be alive with Jesus in them! You sort of quipped about possibly being accused of espousing what Catholics do. Being Catholic myself, I wouldn't mind seeing you accused of that. Seriously though, I think you do view this "issue," so to speak, as Catholics do. Catholicism teaches that men are saved only through . . . Divine Mercy, however works are necessary in order to exist as a living Christian. Works are . . . the natural outflow of a soul wherein Christ abides. . . .

To Earl Essex: Undated, Broward Correctional

I hope whenever we put names together on flyers or what-have-you concerning pro-life prisoners, and we ask for prayers and support for these individuals and their families, please let's always remember to include Tom Spinks! Please. He has been abandoned by everybody. Even before he testified against Mike, he was shunted away. I really feel for him. He did a tremendous and sacrificial work, and then he broke. God love him. He needs us!. . . . Love.

[Tom Spinks turned state's evidence against a fellow pro-lifer—a Lutheran minister with three children—in order to get his own threatened jail sentence reduced. His objective was accomplished.]

To her mother: 10 March 1987, Broward Correctional

I love you so very much. Thank you for all your wonderful letters and birthday greetings and prayers. Mama, I am so proud of you for refusing probation and the probation fee and court costs! I am wondering why the judge didn't give you the few days in jail when you informed him you could not in conscience accept the probation and costs? If the judge set another date to come back, hoping you will have reconsidered, Mama, I think he is doing this to "bleed" you by repeated trips to Pensacola. You need to tell him you can make no more trips, but if the court sends you the bus fare you'll turn yourself into the court when they designate. Don't let them get away with the abuse and very direct harrassment. Make no more trips at your expense. God bless you for being so strong, Mama. You have set a good example for the others. So many have written me about your example while in jail and now also in court. Thank you Mama. . . . Everyone has been telling me they know where I get my ways from. . . .
Love.

To Peter and Dana Lennox: 18 March, Broward Correctional

I once wrote you about my self-centeredness and self-consciousness, breeding cowardice in situations where I am most needed to reach out to others and share God's love with them. There is not a Christian I know who would not have been able to do a far more selfless ministry in prison than I have. You and Dana would have brought Christ to all around you. Please pray for me that I will grow stronger and more selfless in ministering Christ to others. . . .

Concerning your inquiry as to whether I am a charismatic, of course you may always ask me anything. I am not one, however I have a deep respect for charismatics and I love to pray with them. They exude such faith and love and joy and fervor. I love all forms of prayer and am thrilled to see people pray constantly, in whatever form they can do so best. . . . In Jesus, your sister always.

29 March 1987, Broward Correctional

Numbers are impotent if those who comprise them are not willing to take up the Cross. And not even jail is the real cross—especially as, with numbers, our people would be pretty safe from the threat of jail. The real cross is dying to image-consciousness and being willing to confront the holocaust head-on. Not just at the death camps, but in court and everywhere. To totally refuse cooperation with any aspect of the holocaust and its rancid support system. Forgive the soap-box preaching, but I truly believe this is the way we have to go. We have to step out from safety, no holds, and let each other be our protection in the Body of Christ. . . .

Peter, excuse the vehement way in which I present my views. This is just my personality. I do not claim to have absolute truth concerning these matters of strategy. . . . Certainly, I am always open to discuss any and all of these with my dear brothers and sisters. . . . I also do not feel others with differing views support those views out of compromise with principle in the least—even those positions where I personally feel that the position is a compromised one. And where this appears, it is only held as my personal view of the position—not the position holder. Peter, you are a man of Godly, purposeful, and intelligent action—therefore you may often hold a position counter to mine, out of practicality and conviction, as has often been the case with many of my friends. I may differ in my opinion, but I respect them at all times. . . . Love.

Pro-Life Prayer

Dear God, as your Son's charity for us stands as both a reproach to our sins and an inspiration to holiness, grant His peace to those with the courage to identify their very lives with the victims of abortion. Grant us the courage and freedom to follow their example; the grace to be less confortable with our comforts while the daily holocaust of the unborn continues; the wisdom to know that this nightmare will not end as long as we cling to our privileges while the unborn are denied their very lives; and the humility to offer our own lives in solidarity with the unborn—since if we cannot stop the killing everywhere, we can at least stop it in our local centers, until we are ourselves killed or jailed.

To Fellow Rescuers: 31 March 1987, Broward Correctional

If we think that a little jail time is too high a price to pay, let us ask ourselves whether our numbers would be the same if the police were to bludgeon us on the head as we approached the doors of the death camp to block death. Would our people keep approaching the doors? I think they would. In fact, if the price to be paid became higher, I think our numbers would swell. But only if the few now remain resolute, and suffer the consequences first. Then more would be inspired. Now is the time for the committed to show this courage as we face new challenges and commitment.

It will take sacrifice and courage, and most of all stepping out in faith. Our people have that in them to take this step. And our leaders must instill the courage in us and logic of this necessity to move forward to embrace a deeper commitment. We must move into the area of civil disobedience in order to act out Biblical obedience. . . .

Dear fellow rescuers, you are constantly in my thoughts and prayers, in my heart and in the depths of my love for Jesus. May Our Lord and Savior watch over you and lead you most lovingly and gently on the path of His will, and may you and I follow unhesitatingly wherever it may lead. Holy Mother of God, dearest Blessed Virgin, be our comfort along the way. Your sister in Jesus and Mary.

Unsigned Pro-Life Memo to Joe Wall: Undated

The best way—the only way in the long run—to get Joan out, is to join Joan in. And not as a political tactic, not a rational calculation (such as: yeah, well, if we get a thousand maybe that'll do it) but rather for each of us to get a grip on the work we are presently doing, and do it well: but all the while preparing in our hearts, always, to say no. To say, the killing of these children must be stopped, and if it cannot be stopped, then you shall have to kill me too. You are going to have to kill me or jail me, or do whatever you have to do, as of today I say no to this, more than I say yes to other things that are important to me.

I am ashamed this was not understood earlier, Joe, but [I am] overwhelmed that the insight—not to mention the woman!—has been given to us at all. It is so Catholic (with all due admiration to Evangelicals and everyone else). It is like the difference between all the marvelous social programs and Mother Teresa going out to rescue her first dying man on the streets of Calcutta.

From the Holy See

His Holiness Pope John Paul II has received your letter ... 25 February 1987. Monsignor G. B. Re, Assessor, Secretariat of State, Cardinal Casaroli's office, Vatican City.

From Joan Andrews to Michael Lennox:
2 April 1987, Broward Correctional

You know something, Michael? When I first wrote you, the very first time, I didn't realize just how extremely smart you are. I didn't know you'd be able to understand my letters. But wow! You not only understand my letters, but you know about all kinds of things, some of which even I don't know about. Like the difference between a watch and a clock (I do know that), and you know how to explain what jet contrails are. Michael, I couldn't explain that if I tried with all my might. So you see, you are "bigger" than I am in some ways. You know some things that I don't. . . . May Jesus bless you and keep His dear arms around you, as He cares for your every need and happiness. All my love, in Jesus.—Joanie

To Joe Wall: 4 April 1987, Broward Correctional

Concerning the shackles when I was taken to the ocularist, please don't make a fuss about it. A prison has to abide by such strict regulations. Those officers risk their lives when they go on the road with inmates. This is a maximum security prison with people convicted of violent crimes. Individual officers can't take it upon themselves to decide who should and who shouldn't be shackled. Even a prisoner who is incarcerated for a non-violent crime, as you know from jail experience, is capable of possible violence if facing some years in jail. I've known inmates who escaped when they had less than a year left to serve. So please don't get upset with, nor judge the prison. . . . Besides, the shackles are no big deal. Nothing is as painful and brutal as incarceration itself, and separation from family and friends. This latter is the real agony of prison. And yet all of this is to be offered to our Dearest Lord—so how can we, any of us, complain? . . . Yours in His Love.

To Presbyterian Pastor D. James Kennedy:
7 April 1987, Broward Correctional
Especially I am thrilled by your plans to reach out decisively to the Christian community with the message for active involvement in fighting to end this dreadful holocaust. . . . Thank you, Dr. Kennedy, and God bless you for your tremendous leadership and direction.

I think the greatest problem we have faced in the prolife movement has been the view that this work is a separate entity from the Church, the Christian community and from one's basic Christian duty. Surely this duty is based on fundamental Christian love and justice, and is imperative to all Christians living amidst a holocaust.

However, the individual Christian has not seen this truth. I believe this has come about because we have lacked leadership from those who represent the Church authority to us. I think the priests and the pastors hold the keys to the ending of the killing of the babies, but have neglected to use them. If the priests and the pastors could reach the hearts of the multitudes of Christians and lead them to loving, prayerful action in the confrontation of abortion, we might see an end to the holocaust in this land. . . . In Christ.

Letter from Edouard Cardinal Gagnon, President
Pontifical Council for the Family, 9 April 1987
Thank you for your letter of February 26, 1987, in which you brought to my attention the sad plight of . . . Joan Andrews. You did well by informing His Holiness. With every

prayerful best wish, I am . . . Sincerely in Jesus and Mary.

Letter from Joan Andrews to Jeff Frye:
13 April 1987, Broward Correctional
Also, of course, I am grateful to be able to receive a 20 minute visit usually once a week in my cell from the prison chaplain, a priest named Fr. Santos. He is a very good priest and he brings me the sacraments. One last thing. Since you have shared with me so many of your interests, like sports, and literature, but most especially your Christian fellowship, and also because I discern that you seem to be game for any-thing—I have a bargain to make. When I come to Kansas City, if you will teach me some Greek pronunciations, par-ticularly "Chairein in Christo," I will teach you how to ride a horse. You'll be a great horseman. And as you said and I firmly believe, you can do anything that a sighted person can do. How about it? I know neither Greek nor German.

By the way, do you dance, Jeff? I can't to any of the fast dances, but I enjoy the very slow dancing. Maybe a group of us activists can all go dancing together some evening. We do this in Philly at a place where they have all those great old tunes like "Deep Purple," "Moon River," "On the Street Where You Live," "The Summer Wind" "A Stranger in Paradise," etc. It's great fun. . . . God bless you and keep you, my dear faithful Jeff. Chairein in Christo, and the Blessed Virgin, Your fellow rescuer.

To Diane Bodner: 13 April 1987, Broward Correctional
Well, I'd better run before I get fired from my elevated position of Prolife Jail Symbol. It was so nice of the courts to give me this symbolic platform. Such gentlemanly coopera-tion, the wonder of it, it never ceases. But I don't think they will put up with me falling any further behind in my work, so I bid adieu for now. (Maybe I can put upon the kind graces of the aforementioned gentlemen and procure a secretary

for my needs.... Would you rush right down and apply
please? Your bunk is being readied.... Oh I can't wait!
We'll be bunkies again, and I'll have you lullabye the whole
Confinement block to sleep every night!!.... Love.

*Article by Scott Eyman in Sunshine, the Magazine of South
Florida: 19 April 1987*

She dropped out of college and adopted an itinerant
lifestyle, travelling around the country to attend pro-life rallies, working as a domestic or exercising horses. She made no
more than $1,000 in any given year. She mostly lived with her
sister Susan Brindle and her husband, baby-sitting for their
growing brood. And, like the other women in the family, she
began doing what she referred to as "rescues."

Joan Andrews' raids on abortion clinics were fairly ritu-
alistic. She walked in the front or back door and told the
waiting women that they were making a terrible mistake.
And sometimes she attempted to unplug surgical equipment,
with the idea of rendering the clinic incapable of operating
for the rest of that day. Sometimes the rescues worked and
Andrews would convince a woman to forego the abortion.
At one time, Susan Brindle had three such girls living with
her. It was on one of those rescues that Joan Andrews came
to the Ladies Center in Pensacola in March 1986....

In late September, with the judge calling her
"unrepentant," Joan Andrews was sentenced to five years in
prison.... Although Judge Anderson has refused to comment on his sentence, his remarks during the trial provide a
capsule version of his point of view. "You stand before me
today telling me you are above the law," he told Andrews,
"that the law does not apply to you because you believe certain things.... By your criminal action and your criminal
conduct, you have blackened the name of that cause so that
the really responsible, sincere Christians who support that
position have stepped into the background and have sort of

abandoned the cause. . . . "

Tom Bush of Ft. Lauderdale, Andrews' new attorney, is fairly confident that, in a few months, he can get the sentence reduced to time already served because of what he believes are the irregularities in the case. "If we exhaust legal procedures, then I'll petition the governor for clemency," says Bush. . . . [W]hile the hand-wringing and legal manueverings continue, Joan Andrews sits in solitary confinement, secure in her beliefs. . . .

She could be a pretty woman, but she is beginning to look worn and old beyond her 38 years. She bears her afflictions with a joyful grace. . . . She admits that . . . from the time she was 11, all she wanted to do was get married and have children—and yet she never kissed a man until she was 33. She lost her right eye to cancer six years ago and has a glass replacement. . . . She dismisses the difficulty it causes her: "I have to be careful going down stairs."

To look at her is to see someone rare, someone who has willfully chosen to mortify, not merely her flesh, but her entire life. The unspoken logic is crushingly simple: If the babies with whom she identifies so strongly are unable to have a life, then neither will Joan Andrews. . . .

"I have drawn only one line for myself: I will not ever do violence to any human being". . . .

The basis of Andrews' non-cooperation is her feeling that, by sentencing her, the judicial system announced that the lives of the unborn children were not worth defending—and that, were she to cooperate with her jailers, she would be implicitly agreeing with that evaluation. To cooperate with her sentence would, in effect, be to admit her guilt.

She is a glowing, articulate presence; her words rush out, her fingers skittering nervously through the air. Her religious feeling is intense, but she lacks the holier-than-thou arrogance of so many pro-lifers. "There is a spiritual side to non-cooperation," she says. "It has a great deal of power. But, taken too far, passive resistance cooperates with evil. I believe that all humans are as valuable as I am. . . . [E]ven if I had been sentenced to 30 days instead of five years, I wouldn't have cooperated."

It is probably a good thing that Joan Andrews never felt the call to become a nun, for above everything else, a bride of Christ must obey the dictates of the church, and this is a woman resolute in her will; she will obey her conscience and nothing else, and that conscience states that prayer without action is futile.

Joan has not always been the Happy Warrior of the pro-life movement. In 1978 and '79, the constant living out of a sleeping bag, traveling on buses ("You can get shoes at Goodwill for 10 cents; nice ones. . . . ") rooming for a few weeks at a time with other pro-lifers in the network, seeing her family for only five or six days a month, began dragging her down. . . . Her zeal had been renewed by the time her eye, initially damaged when a horse kicked it, developed a malignant melanoma. The eye was removed on a Wednesday and she was back disrupting an abortion clinic on Saturday. . . .

The Rev. Daniel Kubala is director of the Respect Life Ministry for the Archdocese of Miami; he has helped 100 women see their pregnancies to term. Yet he seems aware that, in Joan Andrews' terms, the methods by which he has chosen to serve his church are empty. He struggles to come to grips with her apparently limitless gift for self-sacrifice.

"I neither condemn nor bless what she is doing," Kubala says. "Part of our theology is that God reveals himself to different people in different ways. Outside of the early martyrs, there's not much to compare this to." Is she the 20th century's answer to Joan of Arc, or is she just another religious militant with a private theology impenetrable to outsiders? In short, is she a fool, a fanatic, a saint, or some entirely original combination of all three? "I don't know if that question will be answered in our lifetime," Kubala sighs. . . .

There is no end to it of course. Barring a reduction in her sentence from a friendly Florida Attorney General's office, or a pardon, she will serve her full sentence. Upon her release, she vows, she will "go right out and do a rescue. In all honesty I don't know what's going to happen. . . . When I was having such a hard time, back in 1978, one of the things that brought me out of it was something Mother Teresa said: 'We are not called to be successful, we are called to be faithful.' I realized the truth of that. I just want to be able to say that, when all is said and done, I've done what I could."

And then this intelligent, passionate—perhaps too passionate—woman . . . goes back to her cell. The private Calvary of Joan Andrews begins all over again.

From Joan Andrews to the Editor of Sunshine Magazine:
19 May 1987, Broward Correctional
Regarding the story in your April 19th issue. . . . I was grateful for the kindness and sensitivity with which Mr. Scott Eyman wrote the article, and I appreciate his thorough research and his competence. . . .

There are, however, a couple of points I would like to clarify or correct. [For example] I gave the wrong impression . . . concerning the matter of conscience and Church authority. I am bound in absolute obedience to the authority of the Catholic Church in all matters concerning faith and morals. If there would be a conflict between my conscience and the teaching of the Church, I would unhesitatingly and completely submit myself to the Church's authority. I believe in the infallibility of Catholic doctrine [dogma].

Nonetheless, I agree with the observation that it was best I never felt called to be a nun. A nun takes the additional vow of obedience to her superiors, and this entails all areas and elements of her life, not simply the area of doctrine and moral conduct. . . . Obedience is a great virtue. I hope to practice it in submission to God's will, and were I a nun, I would pray for the strength and submission . . . to fulfill that duty and this vow. . . .

I believe that prayer is never futile. However, I do hold the position that prayer without works is stripped of its strength and power, and, indeed, is less pleasing to God because it lacks service, the manifestation of love. Even a contemplative is called to charity within his or her order and monastery. Not that one has to be active, but simply responsive. . . .

I have the deepest respect for the work of Rev. Daniel Kubala with Respect Life Ministries (Miami Archdiocese), and I hope that he accepts the incredible good his work accomplishes, seen in my terms or anyone else's. There can be nothing empty in that.

Passive resistance to evil can never be taken too far, I don't believe. What I meant to say was that pacifism taken too far can cooperate with evil by doing nothing active to resist it. The distinction being, I believe, that passive resistance always confronts evil (albeit non-violently and with love), whereas pacifism doesn't necessarily confront nor resist that evil which it opposes. Pacifism is more a state of being, as I understand it, while passive resistance is always an action. Forgive me if I am hair-splitting. This is simply my understanding.

The prison does allow me to write and to use the mail. Though writing supplies were restricted and extremely limited at the time of the interview, that has changed and I am now allowed whatever writing supplies I need.

One last thing. I'm certainly not a martyr! I'm just a saint. Or is that fairy princess. . . . ? Or maybe, just maybe, I'm a regular, normal human being who doesn't like to see little defenseless babies dismembered alive. . . . Those who defend life are guilty only of obeying Jesus'command to love thy neighbor as thyself. And St. Paul taught that love does no harm to its neighbor.

Comments by Joe Hart in the Delaware County Daily Times: 29 April 1987

And she's suffered physical assaults in her quest.... Two years ago, at a protest in St. Louis, Mo., Andrews was assaulted by workers in an abortion clinic. "There were five women with heels jumping up and down on Joan but she kept trying to crawl for the suction machine," Brindle said. The workers filed assault charges against Andrews. When Andrews sent photos of her injuries to police in Missouri ... the charges were dropped. Now Andrews is in the deepest trouble she's ever experienced....

From Thomas Daily, Bishop of Palm Beach, Florida to Miriam McCue: 24 April 1987

I am quite confident that Bishop Keith Symons and his staff are looking toward taking care of the spiritual needs of Joan Andrews, particularly because her incarceration is within the jurisdiction of the Diocese of Pensacola-Tallahassee. I will be talking with Bishop Symons soon and shall consult with him. In the meantime, please be assured of my prayers and rememberances at the altar.... Sincerely in Christ.

[Bishop Daily is incorrect on this point. Joan's incarceration at Escambia County Jail, with the priest who thought prolifers "pretty despicable," was under Bishop Symon's jurisdiction. Broward is under Miami Archbishop McCarthy's jurisdiction.]

From J. Francis Stafford, Archbishop of Denver, to Susan Brindle: 27 April 1987

I have received and thoroughly read the situation concerning Joan Andrews.... While I cannot directly comment on the actual situation as you and your family are experiencing it, I want to assure you, as I have many others, that I very definitely support, wholeheartedly, the pro-life efforts of the Catholic Church in the United States, as these are enunciated through the ProLife Committee of the National Conference of Catholic Bishops.

Please be assured of my prayers for Ms. Andrews, as well as for all those involved in pro-life activities in court [sic] with the teaching of the Catholic Church. Sincerely yours in Christ.

[Chicago Archbishop Joseph Cardinal Bernardin is head of the committee referred to by Archbishop Stafford. On 27 January 1988, when Arcbishop Stafford joined Joseph Cardinal Ratzinger and John Cardinal O'Connor in New York to discuss the USCC AIDS document, Archbishop Stafford was informed that Andrews had not heard a Mass for more than a year and a half. He seemed genuinely concerned, and promised to contact relevant bishops on the matter.]

From Joan Andrews to Katie Wirtel:
29 April 1987, Broward Correctional

I was so thrilled when I read in a letter today from your dear mother that you will be receiving Our Blessed Lord in First Holy Communion on May 2! [the feast of St. Athanasius] Oh, Katie, this is the most momentous day in your whole life. How happy I am for you, and how deeply I will remember you in my prayers, especially on May 2, that you are able to know truly in your heart how deeply and totally Jesus loves you . . . and how He has longed for you to receive Him in His Most precious Gift to you. After this special day your life will be changed forever. Every day, if possible, you will be able to come to Jesus and bring Him into your very soul and body. You won't feel the earth shake, but a greater miracle takes place than if the whole world were to shake and Heaven were to appear before your eyes. Because our God, our Lord and Savior Jesus, will come right to you, more closely united to you than He was united to His apostles on earth (except on Holy Thursday when they, too, were privileged to receive First Holy Communion) and closer than He was united to Mary, His mother, except when she carried Him within her womb. . . .

Whenever you are able, dear Katie, please make little visits to the church and kneel in the quiet before the tabernacle where Jesus is. . . . Can you understand how much He loves you? . . . When we give ourselves to Jesus, we receive everything! . . .

When your mother talks of you, her face just glows, and when she writes of you, the words smile up from the paper. You are so deeply loved. One of God's most special gifts to you is your magnificent father and another is your dear mother. Always thank God for them. And pray for them. Moms and Dads need prayers too. And God has a special way of listening to the prayers of little children.

May Jesus put His arms around you as you receive Him often, and may Mary hold you in her gentle care. Wherever there is Jesus, there is also Mary . . . and wherever there is Mary, there also you will find her Son. All my love.

To Jeff Frye: 1 May 1987, Broward Correctional
I just received your wonderful letter of Easter Monday April 20—I am still in the midst of reading it (I'm on pg. 12—concerning your kind and loving defense of Catholics being capable of being true Christians). . . . Jeff, how is it that Christians can be Christians and refuse to pray for anybody? I am referring to that prayer group you left because

they objected to praying for me. Even if they think I'm the most dastardly person (all the more if they think that), why would they withhold prayer? Do they think we are only called to pray for the perfect? Do they not pray for all professed atheists, professed Communists, all people in prison? Sometimes I truly don't understand fellow Christians, do you?. . . . Charien, en Christo.

To Miss Annamaria and her 7th grade class:
11 May 1987, Broward Correctional

Thank you with all my heart for your most wonderful letters. . . . [I]t is hard for me adequately to express just how deeply moved I am by your love and committment to God and to His precious preborn children. God bless you for this faithfulness. I know that Our Dear Lord and His Blessed Mother are deeply consoled by you. You see, so many of God's children offend Him grievously in today's world. But He never gives up on us. He keeps begging us to love Him and to love one another. We are all His children.

Surely, He wants us to defend each other when one or the other is in danger, as the little preborn babies are. These tiny children are being killed in every community in our country today. We must fervently pray for them, and especially for those who cruelly kill them. Please continue to pray for the conversion of all souls to the Sacred Heart of Jesus and the Immaculate Heart of Mary. We must pray that all people lovingly submit themselves to the Divine Will of God and live holy, good lives.

Thank you for being witnesses for the truth by your love of God, your love for the preborn young, and by the powerful example of your own lives. I realize that many if not all of you, are active in prolife ways. By demonstrating against this holocaust in our land, by picketing and counseling at abortion mills, by speaking the truth to adults and young people your own age concerning the evil of killing babies. Thank you for doing what God leads you to do!

John Madden, I was touched deeply by your saying that Mr. Mahoney was lucky to have a friend like me. . . . The ideas that you, Pradeep Varghese, brought up in your letter concerning how to fight abortion were great! When I get out of prison I hope to do this wonderful work with you! Beth Anne Sykhouse . . . I did draw a picture for you of a group of inmates studying scripture from the Bible together. . . . Kelly Fredericksdorf, I was so happy to hear about your baby nephew [and] the love of his Daddy and Mama. . . .

I wish I could comment in more detail about the tremendous respect for life expressed in all the letters each of you wrote [here follows a list of all the children's names]. These letters, each one, expressed a deep love and concern for all our poor little preborn brothers and sisters . . . and a witness for Christ. I feel very, very happy to know each of you and I am very blessed that I can call you my friends. I hope that maybe some day we can meet in this life, but if not, I am sure we will meet in the Kingdom of Heaven.

God bless and keep each and every one of you. . . . You have a wonderful teacher as I am sure you agree. She, as well as your families, and most certainly the Holy Spirit, have guided you well. May the Lord be always with you, and may the Mother of God, dearest Mary, hold you in her gentle care always. Your friend, in Jesus and Mary.

From the Florida Department of Corrections (Robert W. Mac-Master, Information Services Director): 15 May 1987

Your letter, regarding inmate Joan Andrews, to Department of Corrections Secretary Richard L. Dugger has been referred to me for response. Please allow me to explain the circumstances surrounding her present restrictions on interviews. Ms. Andrews is currently being held in disciplinary confinement at Broward Correctional Institution. While in disciplinary confinement, inmates are not permitted to have interviews with the media. Ms. Andrews and her attorney know this. When Ms. Andrews leaves disciplinary confinement, her interview privileges will be restored.

Inmates are placed in disciplinary confinement for various infractions of correctional institution rules. These rules are enforced to protect the health, safety and well-being of all inmates, as well as to provide for the integrity of institutional security.

I hope this explanation is clear. I appreciate your concern for Ms. Andrews, and ask that you try to understand that restoration of her privileges [for example to hear the regular weekly Catholic Mass at Broward] will depend solely on her future willingness to observe institutional rules. Sincerely.

From Joan Andrews to Miriam McCue:
17 May 1987, Broward Correctional
A priest, the Catholic chaplain, comes to see me at my cell whenever he can to bring me the Sacraments (Confession and Holy Communion). He is a good priest and I am very blessed to have him visit me. Miriam, please do not worry about me. Of course, I do appreciate prayers and always need prayers, but please know that I am doing well, and that I need nothing more. Mrs. Villacorta said that you felt I was ill or having a bad time. Being a weak person, naturally sometimes I get terribly lonely, but that's pretty normal for being in prison. After all, I love my family and I have not seen them for some time, as the prison won't allow it. Despite this, God is good and I am spiritually happy. I am pleased to be here as long as God wants me here. Therefore, do not worry about me.

Due to my stance of non-cooperation, I am allowed no personal property in my cell or in my possession other than that which is allowed through the mail, such as photos. Just the same I am treated well. Mrs. Villacorta has especially been considerate to me.... My pen ran out of ink. I should be able to get another one tomorrow, as the prison is supplying all the writing materials I need now, including pens.... With love, in Jesus and Mary.

Open Letter to Florida Governor Roberto Martinez,
in the Miami Voice, by Magaly Llaguno
of Human Life International: 12 June 1987

As a Cuban-born refugee who is also a citizen of the United States, the beacon of democracy in the world, I choose publicly to inform you that I feel very proud of two persons: one a Cuban, the other an American. The first person I feel proud of is Roberto Martin Rodriguez, a Cuban political prisoner who was freed recently and arrived in the U.S. to a hero's welcome. The other is Miss Joan Andrews, an American citizen who is still in jail in Florida.

Roberto was condemned to prison because of his love for his country and for freedom, Joan because of her love for God and unborn babies. Roberto's only crime was to seek freedom for his country. Joan's only crime was to try to save innocent human lives. Roberto started his "passive resistance" against communism in Cuban jails, refusing to wear the blue uniform used by common criminals. Joan started hers [by] refusing to participate in prison activities. Because of this she is denied visitors.

Roberto refused to be "rehabilitated" and as a consequence he was transferred to a maximum security prison. Joan was transferred to the Broward County prison for dangerous criminals because she refused to be "rehabilitated".... The communist government of Cuba asked Roberto to give up his fight for freedom.... The Judge who condemned Joan asked her to stop rescuing babies from abortion.... Roberto refused to accept freedom when it was offered to him, out of love for his brothers who remained behind in prison. Joan has refused to accept freedom if in return for it she has to stop trying to save the lives of her unborn brothers and sisters. . . .

In view of all the above, Mr. Governor, why is Roberto Martin Rodriquez considered a hero in the U.S., and rightly so, while Joan Andrews remains in jail, surrounded by criminals? How can anyone explain that Cuba's communist government pardoned Roberto, while Florida's government has not pardoned Joan?. . . . Mr. Governor, before you were elected you promised to defend innocent human life. To you we appeal for justice. . . .

From Joan Andrews to Magaly Llaguno:
9 June 1987, Broward Correctional
It made me happy to hear that you think God may want me out of prison in order to take a more active role with my brothers and sisters in the struggle. Oh, I do hope this is God's will. I do ache to join these efforts actively. It breaks my heart to be kept from doing so. Also, I find it almost unbearable not to attend daily Mass. It has been almost a year since I have been to Mass. And of course, I miss my family and friends terribly. And yet, Magaly, I am also truly happy to be where God wants me, if He does want me to remain here. And He continues to sustain me. So how could anyone in their right mind ever wish to be anywhere other than where God wants them?. . . . Pro Vida.

From Bishop Thomas V. Daily of Palm Beach to Miriam
McCue: 17 June 1987, Broward Correctional
Thanks so much for your letter concerning Joan Andrews. I will try to follow through insofar as possible. Certainly you should keep your contact with Joan and be kind to her and offer her your support through prayer and your own attendance at daily Mass. God bless you and your family. Sincerely in Christ.

From Joan Andrews to Jeff Frye:
13 June 1987, Broward Correctional

Jeff . . . of that prayer group that refused to pray for me . . . I know they love Jesus, and I feel quite sure in time He—Our Lord—will help them understand . . . in fact, maybe they already do. Possibly their human emotions got in the way when they refused to pray for me. I am sure they meant no malice by it . . . put these dear folks in the gentle hands of Jesus, and they will do well there. . . .

I would really like to learn braille, even more than I'd like to learn Greek. . . . I am still praying very hard that you will reevaluate your position concerning conduct towards the NRLC [National Right-to-Life Committee] . . . or any other group that does pro-life work, but which has an official (or unofficial) stand against Rescue. You see, Jeff, I feel that we must challenge their position on this matter and even fight against it—with love in our attitude and in our hearts—but that we must never fight against nor undermine their prolife labors. . . . Their efforts may not be the best, but at least they are something, and I certainly continue to participate in certain NRLC efforts when I am able . . . because these groups are large and "safe," many join them who would never join us. . . . The abortionists and the anti-life forces are our enemies, not other pro-life groups. . . .

In one of your letters you asked me if I thought the Reformation was necessary. From my heart I must say I regret the break in the Church. I do agree that some reforms were necessary, and these came about to some extent during the Catholic reformation. But I will always wish the Church had never splintered.

Jeff, I certainly think you are right concerning the next victims . . . society will attack. It will be the so-called handicapped. . . . I don't have the kind of courage you have. . . . Yours in Jesus and Mary.

AP Press Release: 19 June 1987

Florida leads the nation in the use of home confinement as an alternative to prison. . . . Bill Dixon of Boynton Beach was sentenced last month to nine years of house arrest as punishment for the shooting death of his terminally ill wife in December 1985. . . .

AP Press Release: 19 June 1987

Gov. Bob Martinez says early releases of inmates will continue at least for the next three months. Further releases will be needed until new bed space becomes available as new prisons open, perhaps in September or October, Martinez and aides said Wednesday. . . . [U]nexpectedly high numbers of inmates entering prison could delay any end to the early releases. The prison system admitted record numbers of inmates in March and April. . . .

From Joan Andrews to William Hickey:
22 June 1987, Broward Correctional

I have not been strip-searched for a long time (I am sure this is due to the kind intervention of the warden, Mrs. Villacorta, God bless her), but when I used to be stripped, all my scapulars and medals would come falling off me as I tried to catch them! Protestants probably think we Catholics wear them out of superstition—especially when they see the multitude I carry! They probably don't realize we simply wear them out of love and affection for Jesus and Mary. And of course, out of consecration of our lives to the Sacred Heart and the Immaculate Heart. . . . All my love, in Jesus, Mary, and Joseph.

To her parents: 23 June 1987, Broward Correctional

David wrote me and I was so thrilled! He told me about some of the courses he is taking this summer. . . . I am glad David is taking some art courses, especially poetry. Psychology seems so introverted and self-centered these days rather than other-oriented and expansive. . . .

Daddy and Mama, it sure would be great to see you. I reminisce a lot about some of the wonderful times together. When I get out, I sure would love to go to Fall Creek Falls with you and Mama for a couple of days . . . do you think maybe we could do this again when I get home?. . . .

Do you think there is a way to get Ruach bred? Maybe Tommy Spence would come over and help you load Ruach so that she could be brought to his stallion and bred? I have the $100 stud fee in the bank you know. I have the extra $100 for my outings with Matt, Will and Glennon [her nephews] already secured, as the prison will give me $100 upon my release, which is standard to all outgoing prisoners (guess they don't want us penniless and heading to the nearest bank in Miami or Ft. Lauderdale for a robbery to cover initial living expenses). . . . I love you so much. Please take care. In the Sacred Heart and the Immaculate Heart.

To Miriam McCue: 24 June 1987, Broward Correctional
Yolanda Brency received the rosary you sent and was just thrilled [and] is grateful for the brochure on how to pray the rosary and is making a real effort to learn it. And after we finish Scripture reading each day, Yolanda prays aloud, and she has begun praying for an end to abortion along with her other intentions. This is such a gift to witness. . . . Yours in Jesus and Mary.

3 July 1987, Broward Correctional
I have just written Rep. [Charles] Nergard. I did not ask him to investigate the prison because I do not think the prison is violating any procedures, and Mrs. Villacorta has been exceptionally kind and cooperative. . . . The state prosecutor has told my attorneys that he realizes the injustices being done in my case, but he has to be as severe as possible

with me because of the pressures "from above" on him. . . . He admits it is all political. . . . Love, in Jesus and Mary.

To Bernard and Adelle Nathanson:
3 July 1987, Broward Correctional
It is my sincere belief that we will not be able to halt the killing, even were we to win a High Court reversal of Roe and Doe and even were we to gain a Human Life Amendment, until and unless our people stop the killing physically with their own bodies. . . . If this is not made clear, if we do not make the protection of children a fact by the obvious means we have always had at hand—our own bodies, our own lives—then abortion will continue barely abated once it's made illegal. It will simply go "underground"—and barely will it have to do that, as the powers-that-be will simply turn a blind eye to it just as they did in the last years prior to 1973. . . .

How I admire and love you!. . . . How the terribly wounded Heart of God must be consoled by your lives—your goodness, your caring, your compassion, your prayer of action in defense of truth. And, oh, how I know He loves you, beloved Adelle and Bernard. God bless you and keep you safe in His arms. All My love, in Jesus and His mother.

To Joe Wall: 16 July 1987, Broward Correctional
There have been several suicide attempts here in lock-up [solitary] the last couple nights. One of the women is wailing right now. A fellow inmate saw her intent and called the officers, and the glass she had broken from the light fixture was taken from her. Last night there were two—one managed to cut herself pretty badly. There was a lot of blood.

The other inmates either react brutally, in a bloodthirsty manner (not unlike the abortionists), egging the victim on to self-destruction or to an attack on the officers, while others call out to her not to harm herself. Then there is cursing between the two factions as they sow their hatred for each other. It becomes utter chaos. Sadly, it's a familiar scene here. . . .

I don't know what I would do without the great blessing of prayer. . . . How I love my rosary, the wonderful devotionals people have sent me, and our rescue hymns and Marian hymns . . . and of course, I feel the prayers of all my family and prolife friends, and you, dear Joe, in such a real and tangible way. . . . I get tired at times, but Dear God keeps bringing me back deep joy and peace. . . . Jesus is always with us. Always, always! And His dearest mother too. We are too blessed to ever truly comprehend fully. It's impossible to comprehend such love. . . . God bless you my dear Joe. Yours in Jesus and Mary.

Story in the Miami Herald by John Arnold: 16 July 1987

Inside the high chain-link fences, razor-wire barriers and the bleak, block buildings of a maximum-security Florida prison, Joan Andrews is doing not only time, but also, she says, the right thing. Solitary confinement in the Broward Correctional Institution is not where you would expect to find a God-fearing, former Tennessee farm girl. Saint or sinner, depending on your point of view, Joan Andrews consoles herself with songs and prayer, passing the lonesome hours in her cell. "It's hard," she explains, "because I'm used to seeing the sky. I was claustrophobic for a while when I first got here."

The cell she describes is painted yellow, not a bright yellow, but a brownish yellow. The only furnishing is a double-steel bunk against one graffiticovered concrete-block wall. She has her choice of upper or lower. The upper is closer to the light of a single fluorescent tube. She can read her Bible on top, near the only illumination she has. Sunlight cannot reach her. The glass of the small window behind the steel grating at the rear of her cell is painted over. This is to prevent her glimpsing the outdoors. Opposite the window and grate is a heavy steel door with a vertical slit. . . .

She is denied visits by her family. And she is not permitted to attend religious services, although she is given communion in her cell by a priest. . . . A devout Roman Catholic, she believes that life begins at conception. In her view, she was arrested for trying to prevent murder. . . .

In her mind, to cooperate in prison is to cooperate with a system that allows abortion. So with the exception of her religious books, she is not permitted to have personal possessions—not a radio, not photographs, not newspapers or magazines—for as long as she is locked in solitary. She can't buy ice cream or a candy bar.

She wears a state-issued prison shirt, blue denim pants, white socks and brown loafers. . . . You might expect a prison pallor, but there is a faint rosiness in her cheeks. Maybe it is the Irish in her. She wears her long hair loose in a girlish style that suits her. . . . She smiles often, and she laughs at herself, confessing that it is difficult sometimes to see the bright side of her situation. "It's important to keep your spirits up and to be cheerful," she says. "People around you deserve to be treated decently."

She writes letters, sitting cross-legged on the floor, a pad pressed against her right knee. Her knee pains her after awhile, but she continues to write, because her knee is her only writing surface. She has no desk or table. . . .

She is allowed a silent hour of walking outdoors daily. Inside, she reads Bible passages to other inmates in solitary confinement, shouting through the slit in her door to make herself heard above the prison din. Often, she is cursed for her trouble. "This ain't no church," some yell back at her.

Joan Andrews knows that. . . .

From Joan Andrews to Jeff Frye:
17 July 1987, Broward Correctional

Jeff, I just thought of something. You know how your collegues at the National Federation for the Blind keep saying that the prolife issue is not a blindness issue? Well, though it certainly is, even if it weren't, why wouldn't they want to support it anyway? If slavery were re-instituted by the courts, would the NFB not want to take a stand against it on moral grounds, even though it didn't relate directly to the blind? Ask them this Jeff. . . .

Jeff . . . when I commented that you were very courageous to have stepped forward at the ACLU debate and spoken so directly and powerfully, I didn't mean it took courage because you are blind. I never even considered that. . . . I think such action, bold and direct, takes courage for anyone. And it particularly stirs me, Jeff, because I am such a coward when it comes to boldly stepping forward and speaking. I am scared stiff to do so, to be quite frank. This is because I have no confidence in my ability to express myself well nor debate well. . . . May the Lord bless you and keep you.

To her parents: 28 July 1987, Broward Correctional

I just finished Bible study and prayer with a couple other inmates through our doors. We usually do this for about an hour each day. One of them learned I had been writing you just before beginning the Bible study and she asked me to give you her regards. Her name is Yolanda and she is more consistent in our Bible study than anyone. . . . Your oldest daughter.

To Bernard and Adelle Nathanson:
29 July 1987, Broward Correctional

Peter told me . . . the remarks you made in Mexico concerning your commitment to the preborn regardless of your personal circumstances. . . . [Y]our love for the preborn, and then for me too, brings tears. . . . When I got back to my cell I just wept. I couldn't help it. It is so beautiful to see the goodness of your heart. . . .

You know what else happened? Just as I was starting to write this letter, I had to pause and wait a moment and look at a couple of pictures I have of Jesus and His Blessed Mother because I had started to cry again, and I couldn't continue. As I did this, a glint of bright orange caught my eyes—so small I could barely be sure what it was. It came from my window, which is painted over so that an inmate cannot see out. The window is overlaid with a large iron grate as well. But there is a spot high up, out of reach from the floor, where the paint is chipped. I had noticed this about a month ago. . . .

Anyway, I . . . climbed up to the crack and peeked out, and, oh, if only I could describe the sunset I beheld! . . . I stayed there until it disappeared, thanking our Sweet Lord for this gift and for the both of you, Bernard and Adelle. I love you so very much. And I pray that you will know God's deepest peace and joy and consolation at all times. . . . Yours with deepest affection.

Letter from Senator Lawton Chiles to Miriam McCue: 29 July 1987

I wanted to thank you very much for your recent correspondence on behalf of Joan Andrews. I am familiar with this case, as are many people throughout the nation. Miriam, I share your concern about Joan. Personally, I am opposed to abortion on demand, and I sincerely feel for her. Unfortunately, in my capacity as a U.S. Senator, I am unable to intervene in a matter of this nature. . . . I do appreciate hearing from you and would be pleased to hear from you any time. With kindest regards, I am, most sincerely.

[According to the annual tabulations of Nellie Gray's March

for Life, Senator Chiles votes pro-abortion roughly 75% of the time.]

From United States Commission on Civil Rights (Neil R. Mc-Donald, Attorney-Advisor) to Miriam McCue:
The United States Commission on Civil Rights recently received your complaint. The Commission was created by Congress to conduct studies, hold hearings, issue reports, and serve as a national clearinghouse for civil rights information. As such, the Commission has no power to enforce laws or regulations, provide legal or direct remedial assistance, or offer an opinion as to the soundness of your allegations. . . . We appreciate the concern and the circumstances which prompted you to write to the Commission. Sincerely.

From the Diocese of Wichita (Fr. James D. Conley, Director, Respect Life Offices) to Susan Brindle:
I received your letter regarding the sad plight of Joan. I was familiar with the story and the tragic display of injustice. Be assured of our prayers for Joan and your family. I have given the letter to Bishop [Eugene] Gerber as you requested. I hope and pray that Joan's witness on behalf of our unborn brothers and sisters will move cold and indifferent hearts. I'm sure our Blessed Lord and His mother are pleased by her heroic efforts. In the Hearts of Jesus and Mary.

From the National Catholic Coalition (Kathleen Sullivan, Executive Director) to Pope John Paul II:
20 August 1987
Millions in the United States are prayerfully awaiting your arrival in our country in September. . . . We humbly suggest a specific action that many feel could have dramatic results. The enclosed is a case history of [Joan Andrews]. . . . Joan Andrews does not belong in prison. Would you please consider visiting her in jail? This could possibly supply the

momentum to free this courageous lady. If you could find the means to adjust your busy schedule to include this very humanitarian act and also request of our President Reagan, who has great admiration for you, that he grant a pardon to free Joan Andrews, it could be a most lasting and profound gesture to help stop this holocaust. Respectfully.

[The Pope arrived in Miami on 10 September, three weeks after this letter was dated.]

From Joan Andrews to Joseph Foreman:
29 August 1987, Broward Correctional

Concerning your thoughts on cooperation and non-cooperation, I agree that certainly this is not an ultimate, is not our goal. But it is a means, a good means, and it also has an element of faithfulness contained within. . . . It would not be objectively immoral for me to cooperate in prison because to cooperate here is much removed from the actual killing, despite the fact that the prison is in a very real way being used to cooperate with the holocaust and ensure its undisturbed functioning. But the reason it would be immoral for me to cooperate at this point is that I do believe God has asked me to take this stand; and thus to refuse to submit to what I feel His Will is dictating, would entail the sin of disobedience. Should I come truly to believe in my heart that God no longer requests this of me, then that would be a different matter. . . .

Of course, I may be misunderstanding God's directives. If so, at least I followed what I felt was His Will. And that is all I am accountable for, in conformity with moral teaching. All I can do is pray, petition the Father, listen, try to discern His voice, and follow that which I feel He is saying. I beg Him to guide my conscience. Then I act on what I perceive to be His will.

I have no other explanations for my actions, Joseph.

However, I certainly understand everything you wrote

on the issue of "co-op" or "non-coop," and I agree with you. One certainly can morally proceed either way. In fact, if I can be candid, I do wish it were in my hands to reason myself out of here. . . . In His Holy Peace.

To Joe Wall: 6 September 1987, Broward Correctional

Joe, please don't be mean. Please, please tell me who the two new couples in our prolife community are. Please?

Well, being a dreamer, I suppose, I kept hoping that maybe by some miracle I would be out before Sept. 18th so I could join the Philadelphia rescuers in Detroit for the rescues there during the Holy Father's visit. I know that won't happen now (unless I get your bilocation study-guide memorized and internalized). . . .

Anyway, I learned on Friday, the day before yesterday, that the Appellate Court ruled to uphold my conviction and my five-year sentence. I had been expecting they would. . . . Despite knowing this, one still tends to hope you know . . . [but] it is only fitting and desirable that we the born who associate ourselves with the preborn, we who love them, are treated with less rights than others. It would be good if all our civil and human rights were taken away. I should be on death row, not merely in confinement. These courts and this society have ruled that all preborn children as well as newborn handicapped children can be placed on death row and summarily executed without so much as a mock trial. So at the very least we should be condemned to death, also, after a mock trial because we love these children and we try to defend them.

I'm not saying it wasn't painful to realize I won't be rejoining rescues again for awhile, or that I'll have to accept separation from all that I love—the Holy Mass, my family, my friends. But if this is God's will, how can I not be grateful? This doesn't mean I wouldn't be terribly happy, too, if Jesus ordains a way to free me before April 1991. If that is

His will, I will deeply rejoice. . . . God bless you, dear Joe. You are always in my prayers and in my thoughts. May the Blessed Virgin Mary hold you close. Yours, in Jesus and Mary.

[In ruling against Joan, the Appellate Court did so "without comment," which legally precludes a further review and appeal of the case to the State Supreme Court. All other motions have been rejected, quickly. Accordingly, except for pardon and clemency, Andrews has no futher legal avenues open to her. Meanwhile, the Detroit rescue referred to above was the final stage of a rescue offensive against the abortion centers in every city Pope John Paul II visited while in the United States. The "We Will Stand Up" campaign——after a phrase of the Pontiff's in defense of the unborn—completely stopped the abortion trade in Miami, Columbia (South Carolina), New Orleans, San Antonio, Phoenix and Monterey, California while the Pope was in these cities. In Los Angeles and San Francisco fewer children, though some, were killed while he was there. Detroit had the most head-on confrontation, and the abortion industry was shut down on that day, in that city.]

From Joe Scheidler to Joan Andrews: 13 July 1987

The message is going to be simply this: come back to us, come back to this movement, no matter how much you may feel that you are doing more good in prison.

I read the article about you in the *Miami Herald*, and it helped me clear up my doubts . . . that the good you were going to do for the movement by being a prisoner has been done. Your time of intense suffering is over and you must, I repeat must, do everything that is necessary now to get out of jail as soon as possible. . . . Nobody would think less of you, Joanie, if you signed the papers they want you to sign, took the tests they are requiring, started gaining time for good behavior and would get out of the place in the shortest possible time. We need you out here. We need for you to give seminars on activism, to be the speaker at pro-life gatherings, to testify with us on the loss of our civil rights, to help reactivate the movement. . . .

I am very selfish, Joan. I don't like to suffer. And your continuing imprisonment causes much suffering. We all feel it. . . . You should be out here saving babies Joan. You should try to get back to your friends and family as soon as possible. You should help us recruit new blood into the movement. You could be invaluable to the movement if you were free. . . . I don't say that the time you have spent in jail is wasted, or that the time you will remain there is not a worthy offering to God. But I believe you have suffered enough for the cause and that your statement, powerful as it has been, has been made . . . but unless you possess absolute certitude that you have to go on with your present program of resistance, I'd say it is time to get this over and come out and give us a hand.

While writing this I got a call from Fr. Markley [the only other rescue activist who has been given a five year sentence so far: but after originally adopting a position of non-cooperation, Fr. Markley reversed it, and was freed after a little more than a year in prison, in the summer of 1987]. . . . I told him what I was writing to you and he said to go ahead and give this advice, but that he will admire and respect your decision, whatever it is. So will I. In the Lord.

From Joan Andrews to Joe Scheidler:
8 September 1987, Broward Correctional
I have prayed concerning all the things you wrote about, Joe. In fact, I pray about those things every day. Oh how I wish I could convince myself that those arguments would be justifiable for me so that I could hasten my departure from here by cooperating. . . . I want out so badly, although there

is no depression in my feeling; simply the deep longing to be with family and friends, and most of all to attend the Holy Sacrifice of the Mass daily. . . .

Please believe me, Joe, I am not doing this in order to stay in prison longer for the opportunity to suffer more. Heaven forbid. . . . the suffering which comes is not specifically chosen, but simply accepted. The most important reason why I cannot compromise is that it is the very issue of compromise—regarding cooperation—which has become the basis and structure and backup of the entire abortion holocaust. I have been as guilty of this as anybody over the years. . . . But if we ceased compromising with the holocaust, we could end it virtually overnight. I believe this, Joe.

Then we come to the practical question—so what if no one is listening? What if that day isn't coming when "everybody" who is prolife will act each day as if it were the only day left in our lifetime to stop the killing—since it truly is the only day left in somebody's unrepeatable lifetime unless we can get in there somehow and save them? Well, then, even so, I would still feel compelled at this point to cease cooperation with evil because it is the only defense I have, and because I am answerable only for my own life, my own actions, to my own conscience, and to God. And, like it or not (and I don't like it much), this view has been given to me—and how can one remain faithful when one perceives a command and yet does not obey? Practical measures are essential—of course—however often it happens that we call certain short-term measures "practical" that in the long term are in fact not practical at all, and which may even be invoked to justify baser considerations (although please don't misunderstand: prudence is the first virtue, and so demands our obedience, a point never to be forgotten simply because—like the word "love" or any other virtue—it can be abused). But in the end faithfulness, trust in God, is the most practical measure of all: and though that understanding too can be misunderstood and abused, I think it is the right understanding of this whereby Christianity has remade the world, precisely as a sign of contradiction to that world's understanding of what practicality entails. The world always wants to slaughter Jews, or Arabs, or the bourgeoisie, or "uppity" blacks, or preborn children, or the "unfit" as Margaret Sanger considered them and her Planned Parenthood still does—as a practical measure to make things easier on a more privileged group of people. And it has always been the Church, sometimes more bravely, sometimes less, that has stood in the path of this "practical" approach. But, Joe, I think it may be true that the world in a particular way needs the Church—needs Christians—to be especially brave today, in order to rescue the world once again from its maniacal understanding of "practicality." Needs this, more than even the shrewdest practical, political calculation—although excuse me since I do believe that faithfulness is incidentally also the shrewdest practical, political calculation.

I am not saying others are conscience-bound to this understanding of noncooperation. Not now, at least. Maybe someday they will be . . . for now, all I know is that I am accountable, to remain faithful in this. I cannot speak for anyone else, and I will always respect the decisions of fellow pro-lifers. . . . I understand that we are not yet prepared to act in unison and pronounce an absolute *no* to any of the killing. But I do think that time is coming when that will be expected of us, when we will have to insist that there will be no distinction between the victims, and we, their defenders—and I believe we will be prepared and willing when that time comes. . . .

God bless you, dearest Joe. You are always in my prayer and heart. Pax Christi.

*Statement from the Catholic League for Religious and Civil
Rights (Walter Weber, Associate General Counsel):
8 September 1987*

Miss Andrews should be permitted to attend Mass regardless of her willingness or unwillingness to "cooperate"
with prison officials. They could not deny her food and drink
as punishment for resistance; nor should they be able to
deny her spiritual food by imposing a religious punishment.

*From Joseph Cardinal Bernardin to Peter Lennox:
9 September 1987*

I am very sympathetic to your request which is known to
those responsible for the Holy Father's visit. At this late date
it is not possible to make any change in the itinerary. Every
moment of these visits is planned months in advance and involves the coordination of efforts of many thousands of people. I am confident you understand. With cordial good
wishes, I remain, Sincerely yours in Christ.

[Cardinal Bernardin is also head of the Pro-Life Activities
Committee of the National Conference of Catholic Bishops.]

*From Archbishop John Foley to Miriam McCue:
12 September 1987*

Thank you for your note and the enclosure received today. By now the Holy Father has already visited Florida. I
assure you of my prayers for you, as well as for Ms. Joan
Andrews. Sincerely in Christ.

[Archbishop Foley, who comes from the Archdiocese of
Philadelphia, is now head of the Pontifical Commission for
Social Communications in Rome.]

From Msgr. John Woolsey, Director, Office of Christian and Family Development, Archdiocese of New York, to Peter Lennox: 14 September 1987

Cardinal O'Connor has asked me to thank you for sharing information regarding Joan Andrews. Have you had a chance to discuss Joan's case with Father Edward Bryce, the Executive Director of the Bishop's Pro-Life Committee? If not, I suggest it might be worthwhile. Let us pray for Joan and all who courageously defend human life. Sincerely.

[Shortly after this letter, Fr. Bryce retired. To date Cardinal Bernardin has not felt it necessary to appoint a replacement.]

From Joan Andrews to Miriam McCue:
19 September 1987, Broward Correctional

Yesterday afternoon Mrs. Villacorta called me for a conference with her. We spoke at some length. I am convinced that she is sincere in her actions. And also, I know that she does try to help me. I think the main problem is the same as with many public officials—they feel they must follow technical codes instead of making common-sense or morally based decisions. It may be that Mrs. Villacorta feels her decisions concerning having orders directed at me monthly to cooperate (which I always refuse and thus incur more punishment and penalties) is a moral action on her part and on the part of the prison.... (Also, the decision may originate in Tallahassee and not with Mrs. Villacorta).... I tend to believe she is sincere. Which in itself is a breath of fresh air after encountering a vast number of public officials and people in the judicial system who are out and out insincere, and dishonest.

At any rate, I did try to point out that it made more sense to refrain from ordering me to cooperate and simply to leave me be—in which case I'd be released from prison on good behavior within a few months . . . the complicity of the prison is deepened by ordering a rescuer to violate her conscience and cooperate with a system that holds the sanctity of children's lives in contempt. By ordering me to cooperate, I must refuse anew each time, and the prison then punishes me anew by taking 60 days good-behavior "gain-time" from me each month. . . . It is a technical code I am violating, but officials often adhere blindly to these despite the fact it is precisely these that make the holocaust possible. At any rate, this will force me to be held in prison for the full five years.

I think Mrs. Villacorta understands my position, and I understand hers. And, as I said, I do think she is completely sincere in her inability to depart from technical procedure—I also think she would like to help me if she could. In fact, in some matters she has bent rules to help me, such as letting me see my mother after the fifteen months of forced separation. . . .

The biggest point is that, though I still am not allowed to be taken to the Mass on the compound to attend each Saturday, Mrs. Villacorta has said that she would allow the priest to say Mass inside my cell for me!! I spoke to Father Mark Santos today, the priest here at Broward, and he said he would try to manage it when he could. So at long last, after 14 months without, I will be able to attend a Mass again!. . . . I spoke with the priest and he feels there is a definite case to be made in Florida for the greatly unfair and disproportionate lack of Catholic prison chaplains compared to Protestant. Out of over 100 chaplains in the state of Florida, only two are Catholic. . . . Love, in Jesus and Mary.

To Joe Wall: 30 September 1987, Broward Correctional
I think I have been getting a disproportionate amount of coverage and aid. I met with Peter Lennox a week ago and he agreed to transform my defense fund into a general fund for all jailed rescuers . . . under the name "Defenders of

Life." The "Joan Andrews Defense Fund" has bothered me since its inception. . . .

But I do have some wonderful news. I should be attending my first Mass in 14½ months sometime in the near future. The priest, Father Santos, was given permission by the prison to celebrate Mass in my cell. Isn't that incredible? I am so happy!! . . . In Jesus and Mary.

To Pope John Paul II:
1 September 1987, Broward Correctional
We thank you for coming to our country. Most of all I want to thank you with all my heart for your tremendous leadership and example worldwide and among all peoples in defense of human life. Your love for all God's children, preborn and born, is a brilliant light reflecting God's Truth and His overpowering Love in this dark world. Your love for the brutalized preborn young is an active love, a true love, a sacrificial love, as you have held out to all people the courageous response that "We Will Stand Up" whenever innocent life is threatened. Thank you and God bless you, our Beloved Pontiff. You are the greatest gift the Holy Spirit has given the world during these troubled times. You are constantly in my prayers and in my heart. I love you completely and I thank God for you. The Holy Church will triumph, and Our Lord has given us you, Dearest Father, to ensure that His Perfect Will is honored, His Holy Truth is served and defended!

It is hard to find words to write you. What words are there to express one's feelings for our Beloved Pontiff? Whatever I might say would be incredibly inadequate. I just want you to know that I love you so very, very much—totally and completely. My whole family asked me to give you their love, Holy Father, and all those who love God also love you who are His representative on this earth. I embrace you with all my heart, with all my prayers, in obedience, in love, and in service.

I have heard that some people have written to you to request that you come and visit me in prison, or that you mention me when you speak. I do not wish this, my Beloved Holy Father. I know you will continue to ask all people of God to truly love the preborn babies who are dying brutal deaths. True love demands a sacrificial abandoning of one-self for the protection of another, the endangered. True Christianity, unconditional love, speaks of dying for the beloved of God—and who can be more beloved of God than innocent, defenseless children? Therefore, I do not wish any-thing other than what you are already doing: and that is pro-claiming true, sacrificial love for our preborn brothers and sisters in Christ—that we may be sacrificial victims for them, and thereby that they might live. Please God!

My Pontiff, my Dear Holy Father, may our Great and Mighty God bless you and keep you safe and full of peaceful joy, and may the Blessed Virgin Mary, Our Queen and Our Mother, hold you tenderly and lead you in the footsteps of her Son.

With all my love and gratitude, your unworthy servant, advocate, and daughter. In Jesus and Mary.

Pope John Paul II's Farewell Remarks to the People of the United States: 19 September 1987

Mr. Vice President, dear friends, dear people of Amer-ica. Once again God has given me the joy of making a pas-toral visit to your country, the United States of America. I am filled with gratitude to Him and to you. . . . I thank all of you from my heart for the kindness and warm hospitality that I have received everywhere. . . . I take with me an unforget-table memory of a country that God has richly blessed from the beginning until now. . . .

Your deepest identity and truest character as a nation is revealed in the position you take toward the human person.

The ultimate test of your greatness is the way you treat every human being, but especially the weakest and most defenseless ones. The best traditions of your land presume respect for those who cannot defend themselves. If you want equal justice for all, and true freedom and lasting peace, then America, defend life. All the great causes that are yours today will have meaning only to the extent that you guarantee the right to life, and protect the human person.

Feeding the poor and welcoming refugees, reinforcing the social fabric of this nation, promoting the true advancement of women, securing the rights of minorites, pursuing disarmament, while guaranteeing legitimate defense: all this will succeed only if respect for life and its protection by law is granted to every human being from conception until natural death. Every human person, no matter how vulnerable or helpless, no matter how young or how old, no matter how healthy, handicapped or sick, no matter how useful or productive for society, is a being of inestimable worth created in the image and likeness of God. This is the dignity of America, the reason she exists, the condition of her survival, the ultimate test of her greatness: to respect every human person, especially the weakest and most defenseless ones, those as yet unborn.

With these sentiments of love and hope for America, I now say goodbye in words that I spoke once before: "Today, therefore, my final prayer is this: that God will bless America, so that she may increasingly become—and truly be—and long remain—"one country, with liberty and justice for all."

Letter from the Florida Office of the Attorney General (Carolyn M. Snurkowski, Director of Criminal Appeals) to Diane Bodner: 8 October 1987

This is in response to your recent correspondence regarding the case of Joan Andrews. Pursuant to Article IV, Section 8 (a) of the Florida Constitution, executive clemency matters require the approval of the Governor and three members of the Cabinet. . . . Thank you for contacting this office. Sincerely.

Report in National Catholic Reporter: 9 October 1987
  Pope John Paul II used "confidential channels" during his U.S. visit to appeal for clemency for an 18-year-old woman on Indiana's death row, a Vatican spokesperson said recently. But a state official said last week the governor had still not seen the appeal. Vatican press spokesperson Joaquin Navarro-Valls said Sept. 26 that the pope sought clemency for Paula Cooper, awaiting execution in Indiana for a murder she committed when she was 15. Navarro-Valls said the pope, through "confidential channels," had made his views known Sept. 17, but did not specify what those channels were.
  Indiana Governor Robert Orr had received no such message from the pope as of Oct. 1, said his press secretary, Dolyne Pettingill. "We have not received anything in an official or an unofficial way," she said. Cooper was sentenced to death after pleading guilty to stabbing 78-year-old Bible teacher Ruth Pele to death with a butcher knife in 1985. She appealed her sentence and asked the pope in a letter sent by her lawyer for help in having her sentence commuted. Cooper is one of 32 persons on death row for crimes committed while under the age of 18.

[As late as October 1987, despite the September letter to the contrary from Father Woolsey above, John Cardinal O'Connor did not know who Joan Andrews was. His press secretary later told me the Cardinal had simply forgotten. That is doubtless true, but it also suggests that the matter was not brought fully to his attention; and if that is true of the Cardinal, so might it have been of the Pope. Governor

Martinez nonetheless did meet with the Pope on 19 February 1988 at the Vatican. Curial cardinals were directly contacted by the American Life League and others, asking that the Pope address the Andrews matter with Martinez. How the Governor will respond to this "confidential channel" remains to be seen.]

From Joan Andrews to Richard Cowden Guido:
10 September 1987, Broward Correctional
You had me laughing so hard reading your last letter that I was spouting tears. I must say it was a strange sensation to hear myself laughing all alone in my cell. . . . The sound was startling. . . . Haven't been unhappy—just haven't had occasion to laugh often. I'm quiet as a church mouse in here a hundred percent of the time—indeed, everyone forgets I'm here and that the cell is actually occupied. If anyone heard me laughing, I am sure they may have feared something inordinate and perhaps dreadful, like a crack-up, had happened to me. The prison psych is always dropping by my cell warning me about that happening one of these days. . . .

In the past I have been known to refer to myself as a "bum" due to the fact that I often travel around the country with a paper bag for luggage heading to jails here and there, in "bag lady" fashion. However, once it got on tape, which I never meant to happen. How my dear mother would cringe if she heard that. She has always instructed me to behave with dignity and never to even joke about being a "bum." So you can imagine my chagrin when Joe Wall introduced me to speak at the PLAN convention in April of '86 by repeating my words to him: "The bum is back.". . . . In Jesus and Mary.

Report in Miami Herald: 25 October 1987
About 75 people, including the creator of the controversial film *The Silent Scream*, picketed South Miami Hospital on Saturday, protesting the hospital's policy allowing

abortions. Organized by the Christian Action Council, a national anti-abortion group, the protest was meant to pressure the hospital's board of directors into banning abortions and to publicize its battle for clemency for anti-abortion activist Joan Andrews. . . . Dr. Bernard Nathanson, who created the anti-abortion documentary *The Silent Scream*, came from New York to show his solidarity with protestors and to exhort them to continue their nonviolent activism. . . .

From Archbishop John Foley (Pontifical Commission for Social Communication) to Joe Wall: 26 October 1987

Thank you for your letter of October 1 regarding the imprisonment of Ms. Joan Andrews. I have submitted the documentation you sent me to the authorities here, requesting them to bring the case to the notice of His Holiness. Sincerely yours.

From Senator Bob Graham to Miriam McCue:
30 October 1987

On the issue of denial of religious services, however, I have written to Richard Dugger, Secretary of the Florida Department of Corrections. When I was Governor, it was my impression that policies had been adopted to allow for appropriate religious observances for all prisoners. I will write you again when I hear from Secretary Dugger. With kind regards, Sincerely.

[As of 1 March 1988 Senator Graham had not yet followed through on his inquiry.]

Letter from the U.S. Department of Justice (Georgia McNemar, Attorney, Office of Enforcement Operatons, Criminal Division) to Miriam McCue: 4 November 1987

You state that Miss Andrews is not allowed to attend Mass and is being deprived of her religious rights. You believe she should be permitted to attend Mass and church and have expressed your views to the prison warden, but were not satisfied with her explanation. You are now asking for our help.

As you know, we do not have a role in sentencing and imprisonment of individuals convicted of state offenses. Miss Andrews' imprisonment is within the jurisdiction of state officials. You may, therefore, address any inquiries about the terms of her imprisonment to the Florida Department of Corrections. . . . I am sorry, but we cannot be of assistance to you. Sincerely.

From the Florida Parole and Probation Commission (Ray E. Howard, Director, Clemency Administration) to Miriam McCue: 9 November 1987

The parole Commission has no jurisdiction to consider an inmate for parole who is sentenced under sentencing guidelines. Joan Andrews is, therefore, ineligible for parole consideration.

At the present time, the award of gain time or time off for good behavior, is very liberal in the State of Florida. Most inmates can serve a sentence in less than 50% of the time specified by the court. Unfortunately, Ms. Andrews is engaging in conduct within the prison system that prevents any significant early release under this provision because of her misconduct. It appears that she has received 13 disciplinary reports and a loss of 410 days of gain time since her receipt by the Department of Corrections.

The only other alternative for possible release earlier than expiation of sentence would be by the authority of the Board of Executive Clemency. The rules of executive clemency prohibit an inmate serving an active sentence from applying for commutation of sentence unless they are first granted a waiver of the rule.

I would have to emphasize to you that Ms. Andrews' disciplinary report record would undoubtedly weigh against her in seeking clemency. It would be very difficult for the Governor or the Cabinet Members to find merit in commuting a sentence or granting any sort of executive clemency for an inmate who does not follow the rules governing their committment or otherwise evidence effort on their part to merit such consideration. . . . Ms. Andrews can mitigate her situation by qualifying for maximum gain time or time off her sentence by maintaining a good institutional record. Yours very truly.

Draft of Commentary by Richard Cowden Guido for Free Speech Advocates' Newsletter: November 1987

The treatment of [Joan] Andrews after her conviction is what has been provoking comparisons between her and the Russian Catholic poetess Irina Ratushinskaya—whose case has not only been covered in the Catholic press, but in the mainline press as well, including a column by George Will.

About Ratushinskaya, Will noted that "four years ago, at 29, she received the harshest sentence given a woman political prisoner since the Stalin era: 7 years hard labor in a camp for 'especially dangerous state criminals'." It was for her opinions that she was convicted, in particular her shamelessly Catholic poetry. As with Andrews, Ratushinskaya was promised reduction and elimination of her sentence if she would just show repentence. To quote Will again, "isolated, tortured, harassed, starved, exhausted, frozen, she could at any time have won release by signing an acknowledgement of 'guilt.' She never considered that."

Due to warming relations between Washington and Moscow, Ratushinskaya was released last December. The comparison between the two Catholic women does not end with the analogy of the opposition to their opinions; the violation of formal law by the state to achieve political ends; or the contempt for justice demonstrated by the brutality of the sentences in relation to the alleged crimes.

There is also the matter of torture. During her four years in prison, Ratushinskaya was beaten, force fed during a hunger strike, and subjected to solitary confinement. Andrews has now been in jail over a year and a half. Because, like Ratushinskaya, she has refused to grant the validity of her accusers' position, Andrews has been put in solitary confinement, stripped naked in front of men in order to be "searched," sent to the maximum security Broward Correctional prison, and put in with the most dangerous female prisoners there, where a prison guard not so subtly suggested she might be killed if she did not abandon her position of noncooperation with the legal authorities. . . . She is not allowed to attend Mass.

From Joan Andrews to Bernard and Adelle Nathanson:
11 November 1987, Broward Correctional
I can't tell you in words how very much your visit meant to me. It was just wonderful! . . . Oh, and how tremendous it was to see how God is using you both to bring rescue efforts on behalf of the babies from out of the shadows. . . . God love you for leading the Right to Life Movement to acknowledging this reality. . . .

Concerning your being fond of horses, would you do me a very personal favor? My sister Miriam and I used to raise horses, as well as work with them. We sold our whole herd a few years back when we needed money for our prolife work, but we saved our favorite mare, the one I mentioned to you. She is 3/4 thoroughbred, and 1/4 quarter horse. Her name is Ruach. . . . I have asked my parents to find a good quarter horse stallion in order to breed Ruach. The favor I'm asking is that if all goes well and the mare has a foal next year, would you accept the foal as a gift from me? I am sure it would be a special colt because Ruach's sire was the most beautiful and magnificent horse I've ever seen. He was a race horse from the New York racing circuit, almost pure white, and most unusual in every way—intelligent, graceful, gentle, and simply gorgeous, like a dream horse you would find in a fairy tale. . . . My sister Miriam and I co-own Ruach, and she said I could have the first foal. Ruach is the only possession I really have. That's why this is important to me. . . . [I]t's just a horse, but if I could show you my love in a better way, I would. . . .

I had meant to write you, Bernard and Adelle, right after your visit. But things have been wild here for the past several weeks. . . . There were several women in. . . . Confinement who were having it very hard and were in a state of hysteria. Two potential suicides in strip cells, and a friend of mine, Yolanda . . . who is very belligerent. We spent nearly every waking hour talking together or reading the Bible, when she wasn't cursing or hostile. I never could figure out what would set her off. She seemed to find hidden meanings . . . poor Yolanda. . . .

Bernard and Adelle . . . listening to you speak about the work you are doing and especially to see the spiritual dimension of it was truly exciting. I can't remember when I have been quite so happy in a long, long time. I don't think I could be more happy except if the spiritual odyssey would lead you to embracing the Catholic Faith.

Forgive me, I have not said that to anyone before. I know God leads people to where He wants them, when it is the time, and in accordance with their own individual walk with God. I didn't mean to interfere with any of that. . . . [Y]ou are obviously already in His embrace. There is but one God. So you are already there. In your fasting and in your love for His children, you have already acknowledged Him and given Him homage. It doesn't matter on that score whether you become Catholic or embrace some other faith or stay independent. But I hope someday it is the Catholic Faith to which you are led. You and Adelle both. Being Catholic myself, I believe it is the fulfillment of all religions, because I believe it is the deepest and truest gift of God's revealed truths and blessings, especially the great gift of the Mass and the Most Holy Eucharist. I would thrill to see you have these. Therefore, because of this, I do pray that here is where you are led . . . a burning desire in your heart for the Holy Catholic Faith.

I'll not mention it again, okay?. . . . All my love, in Jesus and Mary.

Story by Mary Meehan in National Catholic Register:
29 November 1987

Family and friends of Joan Andrews have launched a campaign to have her released from a Florida prison so she can be "home by Christmas." They are asking Andrews' supporters to "devote December as a month of prayers and letters for Joan," according to a recent press release. They want supporters to write Gov. Robert Martinez. . . . In a Nov. 9 telephone interview, Andrews confirmed that her volunteer lawyers will apply for clemency from the Florida governor and cabinet. When she leaves prison, Andrews said, she will "definitely" intervene at clinics again. She will "spend some time with my family, and I also want to talk and encourage others to do rescues." . . .

Janet Keels, staff assistant in Florida's Office of Executive Clemency, said the governor and three of his six cabinet members must first vote to waive a rule that someone in prison may not apply for clemency. She said the clemency process is used chiefly by those who have served their prison terms and want pardons. If they grant a waiver, Keels noted, there will be a background investigation by the state's Probation and Parole Commission and a hearing by the clemency board . . . [B]arring clemency, Andrews will have to serve her full five years.

[In December, the Florida State Parole and Probation Board

recommended that the Governor and his cabinet grant Andrews the waiver. In early February, the Governor's press secretary, John Peck, told me "his response might be doing nothing at all," which as of March 1st remains the Governor's formal position on the matter.]

Combined report from AP, Philadelphia Inquirer, New York Times (29 November 1987) and the National Catholic Register (13 December 1987)

More than 200 anti-abortion protesters were arrested on minor trespassing charges during a peaceful sit-in that closed a private women's clinic for 9½ hours. Organizers of the demonstration, dubbed "Operation Rescue," said the protest at the Cherry Hill Women's Center on North Kings Highway drew more than 400 protestors. They said it was a warm-up for larger protests planned next year in New York and other major cities.... Pro-choice activists, leaders of women's organizations and officials of the clinic denounced the protest as a violation of women's constitutional right to abortions.... "I'm totally outraged at these kinds of tactics," said Linda Bowker, president of the New Jersey chapter of the National Organization for Women.... The action was the largest clinic sit-in ever held....

Report of Father James Lisante, Respect Life Coordinator for the Diocese of Rockville Centre, in the Long Island Catholic: 3 December 1987

Using public protest, Operation Rescue will peacefully shut down abortion clinics. It will gather several thousand people around abortuaries throughout the nation in an attempt to say "the killing must stop." It will be a prayerful, peaceful and completely non-violent protest. Operation Rescue is a way to save lives.

It will bring people of all races and creeds together to proclaim the sacredness of human life. Some who protest will, no doubt, be arrested. Some may even be roughed up a little. I have decided to join this nationally organized rescue mission. I am frightened. I am not looking forward to being a part of my first civil disobedience. But when my courage fails, I think back to my teachers. They marched for human dignity, they marched for civil rights, they marched for peace. Dare we do less for the children? If you would like more information about Operation Rescue write: Operation Rescue. P.O. Box 1180, Binghamton, New York 13902. Phone 607-723-4012.

Memorandum from T. H. to Rescue Activists: 8 December 1987
The Rescue Movement has just achieved a major breakthrough within the circles of the Catholic Church. As a Catholic, I cannot adequately express my profound joy at this recent development. But even more so as a prolife activist I am pleased that a major moral force wielding immense influence now shows signs of backing our nonviolent direct action efforts. . . .

The Respect Life coordinator for a major New York City metropolitan diocese, Fr. James Lisante . . . has publicly endorsed and committed himself to participate in Operation Rescue. . . . Thus Fr. Lisante becomes the highest Catholic official in the nation thus far openly to endorse Operation Rescue. . . . On December 28, 1985, with the complete support of his bishop, Fr. Lisante brought out 2 bishops, 150-200 priests and 4,000 people to a picket of a local abortion chamber.

On December 6, a very influential Catholic group, Catholics United for the Faith, awarded its Catholic Woman of the Year award to Joan Andrews. To receive the award in Joan's absence was the same Fr. Lisante. . . . In addition Bishop Austin Vaughan, an auxiliary from the Archdiocese of New York (Cardinal O'Connor's diocese), spoke in Joan's honor, calling her "the personification of a question that comes up very often in our country at the present time: is there anything worth fighting for, even anything worth suffering for."

He further asserted that Joan "is entitled to the collective support of us all. . . ."

With the dynamic leadership that Operation Rescue Director Randy Terry has demonstrated, with the dramatic events of November 28 in Cherry Hill, NJ, with these recent Catholic and other Christian leadership breakthroughs, the hope of Joan Andrews' release from prison and the success of Operation Rescue in the spring in New York City have increased considerably.

Remarks from Bishop Austin Vaughan's speech at the Awards Dinner for Joan Andrews: 6 December 1987

It is a special joy to be able to talk to you on a night in which you make an award to Joan Andrews. It seems to me she's almost the personification of a question that comes up very often in our own country at the present time: is there anything worth fighting for, even worth suffering for. Joan's answer is a kind of clear "yes" answer to that in a way nobody can possibly mistake. It's obvious that we have to be different because we accept principles that are not universally accepted in our own society, that are not embodied in the things that are a part of it. What she's doing, what she has done, is a kind of clear proof of that. She is entitled to our collective support. . . . That collective support we have offered so far, it seems to me, on this issue of abortion, in many instances has either not been strong enough or not effective . . . so I am very happy to be part of a program in which Joan Andrews is honored. . . .

Remarks of Father James Lisante, Diocese of Rockville Centre, at Awards Banquet: 6 December 1987

The person we celebrate tonight is a woman who is very

much like Gandhi: who sees injustice, who sees the corruption of the law, who sees the destruction of innocent human life, who sees the same battles that we fought a long time ago for human rights repeated in our age against the most defenseless, the most innocent, the unborn. She challenges us by her willingness to be incarcerated, to do more. . . . This is someone who has suffered incredibly for the Faith. This is someone who has suffered for her moral convictions. This is a brave and courageous woman. . . .

Write to the Governor of Florida, who is a Republican, a nominal pro-lifer, and a Catholic . . . challenge him to be open enough to recognize how unfair, how unjust is this sentence, and to pardon this standing up for a moral principle. If he's a governor who knows what it is to have a conscience, he'll understand what that means and he'll take her out of this God-awful prison . . . [though] Joan may spend a long time in jail. We may not be successful in getting her out of there. . . . That many of us might have that same courage, that's why we salute Joan tonight.

*Award of the Immaculate Conception Chapter of Catholics
United for the Faith:
December 8, 1987 (Feast of the Immaculate Conception)*
The Immaculate Conception Chapter of Catholics United for the Faith presents to Joan Andrews the Catholic Woman of the Year Award, for:

Her encouraging struggle for the Right-to-Life Movement, and her untiring defense of the preborn child.

"I feel God's presence guiding and guarding and loving our people, and their families, as we offer our lives to Him to use as He wills. What greater joy can there be than this? None, surely."—Joan Andrews

From Richard Cowden Guido to Staff of Florida Governor Martinez: 27 December 1987

Though Governor Martinez's press secretary John Peck did not know either that Miss Andrews was in solitary confinement nor that she had not heard a Mass in over seventeen months, he stated for attribution [on 23 December 1987] that "The Governor does not at this time have any reason to believe that the treatment Joan Andrews is receiving from the Department of Corrections is inappropriate." Mr. Peck also suggested that all constitutional questions are matters for the Judiciary, not the Executive, which indicates either a disagreement with or ignorance of nearly all Constitutional opinion. I am sure Governor Martinez knows his authority and responsibility in these matters, but I am not sure he knows all the facts of the case.

Statement from the Office of the Governor of Florida: 26 December 1987

Governor Bob Martinez today agreed to transfer Florida inmate Joan Andrews to the physical custody of Delaware prison authorities so she can serve the remainder of her sentence near her family. The Governor said humanitarian concerns during this holiday season led to his decision, although Andrews' request for clemency remains under review. . . . The Governor said Delaware authorities have agreed to accept Andrews under an interstate compact that is used regularly to allow inmates to serve their sentences near family members who live in other states. Andrews will be transferred as soon as the necessary procedures can be completed, probably within a few weeks.

[On the morning of 26 December 1987 Andrews was transferred not to Delaware, but to Alderson Federal Prison in Alderson, West Virginia.]

7

From Joan Andrews to Tom May:
26 December 1987, Florida Correctional at Lowell

I was at Broward for Christmas, but early this morning, I was transported here. It will probably take several weeks, at least, to reach the Delaware prison at Claymont. It's a nice place. Don't write me here at Lowell because I'll be gone by the time you receive this letter.

I'll write only this one page because the lighting is poor. It's funny how different prisons vary—even the lock-up [solitary confinement] units. What is nice here is the fresh air coming in through the cracked windows, and also the posibility to look out the window and see the sky and even grass and trees. The windows are not painted out here.

My Christmas was great! The priest came by and brought me the Sacraments, and I had a missalette, so after he left, I read Christmas Mass. I had also read the Midnight Mass the night before. I was able to obtain two red plastic garbage bags the night before and I used these to cover my light fixture so that my room glowed. It was beautiful! I sang all the Christmas hymns from the missalette. Then when I was transported this morning at 4 a.m., I saw my first Christmas decorations. Even at that hour and on a main highway, many of the little towns had their Christmas lights on. I got to hear one Christmas song on the vehicle's radio, too. It was a joy.

I can't tell you how good it is to be away from Broward. Jesus certainly blessed me on His birthday. I hope He blessed each of you as much as He blessed me.

AP Release in the Miami Herald: Christmas Day, 1987
Governor Bob Martinez's decision to show leniency toward a woman convicted of vandalizing a Pensacola abortion clinic has been criticized by the National Organization of Women. . . . Her transfer follows lobbying efforts by Catholic organizations to have her sentence commuted—a request that is still being considered by Florida's Clemency Board. Miami attorney Julia Dawson, state Legislative director for NOW, said: "This is an individual legitimately regarded as a terrorist who has tried to block the constitutional rights of the women of this country, who is uncooperative, who is facing other charges and who, if released, would continue to be a threat. To consider any kind of clemency is egregious."

News Story in the Washington Times: 12 February 1988
The Soviet Union has begun a propaganda campaign against Armando Valladares, head of the U.S. delegation to the U.N. Human Rights Commission conference in Geneva, U.S. officials charge. . . . Valladares spent more than 20 years as a political prisoner in Cuba. . . . "This professional terrorist is being sent to Geneva to fight for human rights," exclaimed *Isvestia*. The newspaper also charged that "American propaganda" had falsely turned Valladares into a "prisoner of conscience," a "prominent intellectual" and a "poet who stoically survived the adversities of jail despite the paralysis that confined him to an invalid chair."

From Joan Andrews to Earl and Kathleen Essex:
31 December 1987, Alderson Federal Prison

Well, how about this? I find myself at a Federal prison as a hold-over. . . . This place is a paradise compared to Broward. Tonight being New Year's Eve, they had a bonfire and a sing-along in the big field in front of my cell (I'm in confinement of course). It was really nice. I can't get over my big window with no iron gate and clear glass view, plus I am able to open my window and take in the fresh air. It was lovely tonight, mild and balmy, with the scent of wet fallen leaves, burning wood, and a drift of smoke in the air. . . . All my love, in Jesus and Mary.

Human Life International press release: 28 December 1987

Prolife leaders from around the nation have criticized the decision of Governor Robert Martinez to transfer prolife activist Joan Andrews from Florida's maximum security prison, where she has been in solitary confinement, and have called for her release. . . . The governor has received over 20,000 letters asking for release by pardon, commutation or clemency. . . .

Fr. Paul Marx, OSB [Order of St. Benedict], president of Human Life International, said that "the decision by Governor Martinez of Florida to transfer prolife activist Joan Andrews to Delaware as a 'humanitarian gesture' is neither just nor courageous. He should just let her out."

Prolife leaders calling for release of Joan Andrews include (partial list): Fr. Virgil Blum, S.J., of the Catholic for Religious and Civil Rights; Judie Brown, President of the American Life League; Chuck Colson, Prison Ministries; Richard Cowden Guido, historian, currently finishing a book about Joan Andrews; Rev. D. James Kennedy, Coral Ridge Ministries; Magaly Llaguno, Latin American coordinator, Human Life International (Miami); Juli Loesch, Prolife Nonviolence Education Foundation; Rev. Paul Marx, President of Human Life International; Bernard Nathanson, M.D., currently making a film about Joan; Joe Scheidler, Director of the Pro-Life Action League; Rev. Bob Weiner, Marantha Ministries (Gainesville, Florida); Rev. Donald Wildmon, National Federation for Decency; Rev. Curt Young, Executive Director of the Christian Action Council.

Report in the Wanderer, national Catholic weekly:
7 January 1988
The Tallahassee Department of Corrections [says] the move to West Virginia is just a temporary measure until arrangements can be made to transfer her to a women's prison near her family home in Delaware.... Florida will retain jurisdiction in the case.... Joan will be imprisoned just 12 miles from the family home [of Susan Brindle] close to Wilmington.

From American Life League (Judie Brown) to Fr. Joseph Mc-Fadden (official of the Archdiocese of Philadelplhia):
8 January 1988
Joan Andrew's witness for the unborn through civil disobedience has been explicitly endorsed by: the Diocese of Rockville Centre, whose pro-life coordinator Father James Lisante on Ms. Andrews's behalf accepted the Catholic Laywoman of the Year Award for her on 6 December 1987; and also by New York Archdiocesan auxilary bishop Austin Vaughan, who was the featured speaker at this awards dinner, where he said that Joan Andrews is "the personification of a question that comes up very often in our country at the present time: is there anything worth fighting for, even worth suffering for." The Bishop added that Ms. Andrews is "entitled to the collective support of us all." This teaching is especially significant in light of John Cardinal O'Connor's explicit defense of civil disobedience in 1984 after his auxiliary bishop Emerson Moore was arrested for it in Washing-

ton D.C. that year.

Speaking for Bishop McGann and the Diocese of Rockville Centre, Father Lisante called upon the Governor of Florida to pardon Andrews; calls for this purpose were also put through by, among others, Bishop Vaughan; Palm Beach, Florida Bishop Thomas Daily; Miami auxiliary bishop Agustin Ramon; as well as prominent Protestant leaders. . . . Secular calls were put in by such diverse secular figures as Nat Hentoff, Bernard Nathanson, and Patrick Buchanan, who is preparing a television program on Andrews for expected release [soon]. In addition, the Cable News Network, the 700 Club and the award-winning film company Bernadell, Inc. have either done or are planning programs on Andrews and civil disobedience against abortion centers.

Not least, the American Life League held extensive consultations on the Andrews case with Vatican officials in Rome during the Synod on the Laity. . . .

In light of these facts, and the additional one that Bishop McGann has explicitly endorsed the civil disobedience planned for New York City abortion centers this spring . . . the American Life League must strongly and publicly protest your actions in November against pro-lifers in the Philadelphia area, and against the public positions of leading bishops in the dioceses of Long Island, Florida and New York.

In particular we must protest your phone call to Father Louis Kovaks insisting he could not host Catholics and other Christians who were planning to engage in anti-abortion sit-ins, as he had done many times in the past. What makes this decision especially reprehensible is not only that it further rends the fabric of cooperation in the American episcopate, but that the call was made after, and so it would seem because of, public insistence to this end by proponents and practitioners of the abortion trade (see enclosed).

Father, we find it difficult to believe that Cardinal Krol

approved this policy of open collusion with abortionists, especially one in opposition to the stated policies of his fellow bishops.

Accordingly, given the importance of the Philadelphia See, and the collusion in this policy not only of yourself, but of other leading Archdiocesan figures such as Father John Sibel and Marie Kelly, we hope you will understand the necessity of this protest, the need to make it public, and our hope that you will reexamine and repudiate the policy that provoked it. With God for Life.

From Joan Andrews to Father Lisante:
13 January 1988, Alderson Federal Prison

I do not know how to thank you for the great honor you paid me by accepting the CUF award for me.... Such a powerful and beautiful and utterly kind tribute you gave. I am deeply touched and humbled by your kind and good heart.

Most of all, dearest Fr. Lisante, I thank you with all my heart and the very breath of me for your personal endorsement of rescue missions on behalf of endangered preborn children, their confused and distraught parents, and our dear, afflicted abortionist brethren. Thank you, thank you, and God love you for encouraging others, the many, to participate in the upcoming rescues, by pledging yourself to risk arrest while peacefully intervening and preventing the killing in NYC during Operation Rescue.... God love you and bless you, my dear Father Lisante ... beloved priest of Jesus Christ! Please know that you and your efforts, and your family, are daily in my prayers and small sacrifices, and most deeply in my heart. Yours, with affection and gratitude, in the Sacred Heart of Jesus and the Immaculate Heart of Mary.

To Bernard and Adelle Nathanson: 19 January 1988, Alderson

I like it here at Alderson very much. Wish you could see the view out of my window. It is utterly magnificent. There is a large field out front, treelined roads, red brick cottages (inmate dorms), and high, majestic mountains in the background. I am in lock-up in the confinement unit because as a hold-over between states and between prisons, I cannot be permitted in the prison compound, but nonetheless it does not seem to matter here because my view is so breathtaking and my cell looks more like a room than a cell. In fact, I must confess that I spend endless hours just gazing out of my wonderful window. God has been good to me.

I wouldn't mind at all spending the rest of my sentence here, except for the fact that my family will possibly be able to visit me once I'm moved to Delaware, and I hope, there, I will be permitted to attend the weekly Mass celebrated inside the main building—where, thank God, I will be housed. Therefore, my dear Bernard and Adelle, as you might imagine, I do long for Delaware to pick me up and I keenly anticipate my arrival at a prison close to home.... God bless you.

24 January 1988, Delaware Women's Correctional Institute

I am presently at Women's Correctional Institute right outside Wilmington, about 20 miles from my sister and brother-in-law's home, Susan and David Brindle. It is great to be here. I arrived on Friday evening, January 22, the anniversary of Black Monday of course [the *Roe v. Wade* decision]. It was a special gift to be transported that day, and I asked the two Delaware transportation officers if they'd drop me off at a death chamber in D.C. for a couple of hours since we'd be passing through. But they said they would be giving the city a wide berth....

Disciplinary lock-up here is only 24 hours per incident, so perhaps there will be times when I will be able to have family visits. The officers and staff here have been very kind to me, and are markedly understanding of my non-cooperation, more so than at any other place I have been, God love them.

The only disappointment is that the prison no longer has a weekly Mass celebrated within the building here as they did in 1985 when I was incarcerated. They do, however, have a laywoman who brings the Most Blessed Sacrament, and that's tremendous! Also, I believe they will probably allow a priest to visit and celebrate Mass. . . .

Thank you, my beloved Bernard and Adelle, for your kind prayers, beautiful friendship, and your magnificent efforts for the children! I love you and I hold you in my prayers and in my heart constantly. God Bless you.

Report in the Wilmington Morning News (Gannett):
25 January 1988

The anti-abortion faithful gathered Sunday evening outside the Women's Correctional Center in Claymont in a homecoming ceremony for their captured angel. Joan Andrews, viewed by many as the "Mother Teresa" of the anti-abortion movement, has been jailed there since Friday, following her transfer from a Florida prison. "Joan is the torch of the pro-life movement, an inspiration to all of us," said Dennis Sadlier . . . who founded Liberals for Life. . . . About 50 people came out to support the woman they see as championing a civil rights crusade on behalf of the unborn. . . .

Andrews' incarceration has made her a symbol for the national movement, which has increasingly opted for direct confrontations such as the one at the Women's Health Organization in Stanton [where] seven demonstrators were charged with trespassing and disorderly conduct after they tried to "rescue" patients there. People in growing numbers are willing to face jail . . . said Sadlier, who has been arrested 12 times for entering clinics. . . . Movement leaders plan to lobby Martinez, whose state retains jurisdiction over Andrews, until he frees her. "He hasn't seen anything yet," Horrocks said.

Unsigned pro-life memo to Diane Bodner:
31 January 1987
Don't make the injustice to Joan the key issue. It isn't. The key issue is the murdered children, and her willingness to subject herself to injustice because of what they suffer, which is far worse than what she suffers. It would be a small victory, if a victory at all, to lift the injustice against her without lifting the injustice against them. As I told Joe Wall, it seems to me (just by reading what Joan has said), that the slogan ought not to be Get Joan Out, but rather Join Joan In. That would make our umbrage about the injustice to her, and to the unborn, something people might pay attention to. And something God surely would.

From Joan Andrews to Susan and David Brindle:
27 January 1988, Delaware Women's Correctional
The vigil here at the prison Sunday night was just tremendous. I was in lock and suddenly I heard shouts throughout the building of: "The prolifers are here! The prolifers are here!" My two cellmates were out in population and they told me later that everyone was really impressed by the vigil, and that they explained to everyone why the picketers were there and why I was non-cooperating, and that everyone was learning about the evil of abortion. They said everyone was in support.

Next day the counselor, Miss Johnson, a very nice person, said that the prison just could not allow the picketers to come back again. That the prison would have to have them arrested. I answered, "I don't think it matters if you have them arrested. They could join me in non-cooperation." Her face dropped a little when I said that.

She told me that if I continued non-cooperation and if the prolifers kept coming back, I'd have to be transferred to another prison. I was quiet and polite and not belligerent, but told her this was not something that made a difference to me, or that would influence my decision.

I sure do long to see you! Maybe God will grant me a visit. God bless you.

[On 29 January, Joan's sisters Susan and Miriam visited her in prison, and have done so on subsequent occasions, as have Juli Loesch, Joe Wall, Brent Bozell, and others.]

Story by Mary Meehan in the National Catholic Register:
24 January 1988
Joseph Wall didn't start out to be an activist, much less someone who bounces in and out of jail like a yo-yo, but late last month his many jailings for sit-ins peaked in an indefinite prison term for contempt of court.

Until recent years, the 60-year-old Philadelphian led a quiet life. He attended parochial schools, then studied accounting at Villanova University. He worked 20 years for the city controller's office of Philadelphia and was a senior auditor when he was fired a year or so ago. Wall lost his job when his office refused to let him take vacation time for jail. He has a pension and recently noted that "my wants are few." He is single, which he once said "makes it easier to be a kami-kaze pilot."

By the end of November 1987, Wall had been arrested 33 times. "I shouldn't keep track of it," he remarked, "but I'm an accountant, and I keep track of numbers." He had open heart surgery three years ago. At least twice since, he has been knocked to the ground by abortion clinic supporters. Twice he has collapsed from exhaustion, once after being knocked down.

On Dec. 28 Wall was jailed for contempt of court. He

and Howard Walton, also of Philadelphia, had refused a Catholic judge's order that each pay $1,000 in attorney's fees to an abortion-clinic lawyer. Before going to jail, the two declared that the court "has put us in the position of having to choose between going to jail or disobeying our conscience as Catholics. We choose to obey our conscience. . . ."

A week before his imprisonment, Wall conceded that he was "scared to death" of an indefinite stay in jail. But he added: "They are out to break us, that's the real goal. It's important that Howard and I stand firm to show this tactic won't work." The jailing of Wall and Walton was the latest result of a civil suit an abortion clinic brought against them and 25 other prolifers under a federal anti-racketering satute (the Racketeer Influenced and Corrupt Organizations law, or RICO). The clinic won the case last May; the prolifers plan to appeal when post-motion trials are over.

Judge James McGirr Kelly, who presided over the trial, issued an injunction forbidding the defendent to go on the public parking lot by the clinic in order to protest, picket, chant or leaflet. Wall and Walton continued to do the sidewalk counseling at the clinic. They were charged with violating the injunction, found in contempt of court and ordered not to return to the parking lot. The judge also ordered them to pay attorney's fees to Edmund Tiryak, a lawyer for the abortion clinics [Tiryak was the featured speaker at a National Organization for Women convention workshop shortly after this victory.]

How did Joe Wall get involved in all this? He did traditional prolife work for years. But by the early 1980's he . . . joined others in blocking entrances at clinics in the Philadelphia area. As many as 80 people have been arrested at one time there. Abortion clinics and courts in Philadelphia have reacted sharply against the sit-ins. Stiff sentences, injunctions and the RICO suit have all been used against the activists.

Wall has criticized Catholic judges like Kelly, who he

says have been especially harsh with prolifers.... Last September, after "boiling" over Judge Kelly's verdict in the RICO contempt case, Wall commented: "I only wish I could take these things in the right spirit the way our prolife saints do.... All I do is get damned good and mad, and thereby lose the spiritual benefits of being unjustly persecuted...."

Wall said that being "bored stiff" and the "awful, awful noise" are the worst parts of being in jail. He understands why people who have never been arrested are afraid: "You're stepping out alone, and it's a fearsome thing to walk out in front of the whole crowd." After a first arrest, he said, "You know you can do it. They don't eat you alive. You go through a lot of red tape and stuff, and eventually you get out." He encouraged others to be arrested:

"Don't wait until everybody is doing it, and it becomes a popular thing, an 'in' thing to do. Do it now, when there's a little bit of minor hardship attached to it. This is when we need people."

[Joe Wall and Howard Walton were released from prison, without conditions and without paying Tiryak, on 29 January 1988.]

From Joan Andrews to Joe Wall:
11 February 1988, Delaware Women's Correctional
You are so dear! What can I say? ... Last Sunday when you and the others came up to the cell window, I was so deeply moved and overwhelmed. God bless you and thank you Joe.... The woman who called me over's name is Joyce, and she is facing the electric chair—which the state is determined to seek.... She's a wonderful, wonderful person, one of the two nicest in this prison. Please keep her and her husband in your prayers. Joyce told me to tell you to come to her window any time and give her any message for me, should I not be allowed to get over there the next time, since the guards will be on the alert. But I will always do my best

to be there shortly after 8:00 p.m.

Tell dear Jack that he was so sweet to be concerned about my window being painted over in retaliation for such actions by the prayer vigilers—but assure him that I'd gladly spend the next three years without a window for just one glimpse of him and Pat and you, and all my friends. You tell him, Joe, okay? I was so deeply touched and so overjoyed to see all of you. God love and bless you. . . .

God bless you, my dearest Joe. Please know that you are always, always in my prayers and in my heart. In Jesus and Mary, with love.

Report by John Cavanaugh O'Keefe for Human Life International: January 1988

ChristyAnne Collins left her AIDS ministry to work full-time for unborn children. She began counseling women approaching the abortuary every day it was open. Her approach was direct. . . . In one ten-month period, she persuaded over 80 women to turn away from death and choose life for their children.

The battle for the minds of the women and the lives of the children went back and forth there. In order to "protect" their patients, the abortionists put up a fence at the edge of their property. ChristyAnne got permission from the neighbor (a Catholic church) to erect a platform next to the fence, so that she could still talk to women in the parking lot. The abortionists countered by having their escorts (or "deathscorts") hold a banner up in front of her. . . . [S]he spoke up. To drown out her words . . . the deathscorts began playing their radios loudly. ChristyAnne countered that by using a bullhorn.

The abortionists then charged her with trespassing on their air space. She was acquitted of those charges. . . . [O]n several occasions ChristyAnne led groups in direct action, blocking access to the execution chambers. One of these rescue missions was announced ahead of time, with widespread publicity. The police officer who was going to be responding to the scene on that day (a Catholic) stated that he expected to use dogs to clear people out. He backed away from that threat when a reporter for the *Washington Times* called him to ask whether he was really planning to use dogs on a non-violent group.

The penalties for her activities grew rapidly. On one occasion, she served a 60-day sentence for trespass. During her incarceration, she prayed and fasted . . . counseling prisoners and their relatives. During that jail term, a man charged with assaulting her came to trial. She was brought from jail to testify, and he was convicted. He got a small fine for assault. ChristyAnne returned to jail for trespass.

Immediately after her release, she made it clear that she would not be deterred by jail. She led another rescue mission at Commonwealth. Again, she was convicted: this time, she was sentenced to a year in jail. She appealed, and got a jury trial. They convicted her, but reduced her sentence to a $500 fine (in Virginia, the jury decides the penalty).

ChristyAnne was also charged with "inciting others," in violation of a Jim Crow Law, which had been written to prosecute civil rights activists. The trial happened to land on January 15, Martin Luther King's birthday; the prosecution dropped the charge.

The Falls Church prosecutor, Billy Hicks, is fiercely determined to silence the voice of conscience in the community. The most recent episode began with a relatively quiet day of counseling at the abortuary. ChristyAnne had been speaking for a few minutes to a woman who stopped outside the parking lot. The back end of the woman's car was still sticking out into the road, and a passing driver honked, so the woman pulled a little farther into the driveway. ChristyAnne moved in also, stepping over the property line. A police officer, who had been observing her from across the street, came over and arrested her.

When ChristyAnne arrived at the police station for booking, she learned that she was going to be charged with "interfering with the right to work" as well as trespass. The two charges came to trial separately, and ChristyAnne was acquitted of "interfering with the right to work," with help from the attorney who had drafted the Virginia law under which she was charged. But when the trespass charge came to court, ChristyAnne was convicted, and Billy Hicks asked for the maximum penalty. She was sentenced to a year in jail, for stepping 24 inches onto the property of an abortion clinic during a conversation with a patient there. ChristyAnne is appealing. The court date is 14 January. For now, she is free.

It is difficult to imagine that anyone would miss the point here, but it should be made explicit. People do not go to jail for long terms for simple trespass. . . . ChristyAnne is a threat because of what she says, what she believes, what she represents. She is being persecuted by the City of Falls Church, in the United States, for her religious convictions.

[Miss Collins was offered the chance to accept a $50 fine instead of a year in jail. She said no, she wanted either a jury trial or for the charges to be dropped. As jury selection began the courtroom filled with pro-lifers, and, perhaps because of that, the prosecutor asked that the charges be dropped. The judge accepted the prosecutor's recommendation.]

Report in the Wilmington News Journal: 27 January 1988

Even after 14 years of fighting, Joan Andrews can't believe she has become a national symbol of the anti-abortion movement. . . .

"I was such a coward as a kid," she said Tuesday, sitting in the library at the Women's Correctional Institution at Claymont. Smiling frequently, Andrews spoke quietly while she described herself as timid and peaceful by nature.

"I was so shy I could hardly bring myself to go into a store and buy anything," she said. "I was always afraid of teachers—even nice teachers—and cops. And I don't like to have to talk in public or attract attention, even now. I'm really a terrible spokesman for pro-life."

Yet she has become not only a spokesman but a symbol for many anti-abortion activists. Protestors nationally sent thousands of letters to officials in Florida, where she was imprisoned for almost two years, urging her release. Some have nicknamed her "St. Joan of Newark" for her activism [Newark, Delaware, though St. Joan of Lewisburg might be closer to the mark]. Andrews says she treasures the hundreds of letters she receives in prison, saving them all and answering as many as possible, but she is uncomfortable with the attention.

"When people write to me and tell me how 'saintly' and 'holy' I am, I feel terrible," she said. "I'm no saint, for one thing. I'm just a regular person who happened to be in the right place—or the wrong place—to get arrested. . . .

More than three years remain in the five-year prison sentence.

On Friday, Andrews was brought to the Claymont prison from a federal penitentiary in West Virginia, where she had been held briefly during a transfer from Florida to Delaware. The transfer keeps Andrews under the authority of the Florida officials but allows her to be near her family. In Florida, she was held in near-isolation in a maximum security section of the prison.

"I was kept in a lock-up unit in Florida because I am a non-cooperating prisoner," Andrews said during an interview Tuesday. "When I got here, I talked to the warden and explained that I would be non-cooperating here, too. She was very understanding, but of course she has regulations to follow because she has a prison to run." Despite the apparently mutual understanding, Andrews knows that her refusal to follow prison procedures will mean restrictions on her activities and on her ability to see visitors. And, she said, it probably will continue to mean that she loses any chance to have her sentence reduced for good behavior.

"I didn't want to do it because I know what I'm losing, but the whole idea of not cooperating is to be a burden on the system," she said. "I'm not violent, so I'm no burden in that way, but I'm a symbolic burden. . . . Once you decide to become a burden, you do it with love, but you have to do it with total commitment." Andrews foresees a time when more and more abortion opponents will follow the path of passive resistance. . . .

"Ever since I was a little kid, I've wanted to get married, and I know I'm cutting down on my chances of doing that," she said about her arrests. "But when a war is going on, people have to participate in the . . . suffering."

When Andrews is released from jail, probably in April 1991, she hopes to spend two weeks caring for her sister's children in Newark. But soon afterward, she plans to continue efforts to close abortion clinics—a process she calls "rescuing"—by damaging equipment, or blocking doors or other non-violent means.

"I hate prison, but I know I'll probably be back in," she said. "I'd like to take those two weeks off, but if there is a rescue going on—even the first day I get out—I'm going to go."

Nationally Syndicated Column by Joseph Sobran:
10 March 1988

Our whole society has done a series of flip-flops on what we now call "issues" but which used to be matters of consensus, abortion being the most crucial of them. Many politicians decided abortion was a right rather than a crime about the time the Supreme Court said so. . . .

As I watch [Richard] Gephardt's star rise, I am reminded of a woman named Joan Andrews. Andrews is serving a five-year prison sentence—more than some hardened criminals get—for slightly damaging a machine used to abort unborn children.

You can say what you like about her, but Andrews did what public opinion says Kurt Waldheim should have done. She refused to go along with what she saw as an aberration from civilized life. She couldn't join the general flip-flop.

If Andrews is a "fanatic," Waldheim must be a "moderate"—a reasonable man who goes along with change when it occurs, even if he wasn't on the cutting edge. A chameleon. Naturally he is against Nazism now. He knows when to flip and when to flop.

Gephardt is an embarrassing reminder that most of us are closer to Waldheim than to Andrews. Andrews goes to prison. Gephardt may yet go to the White House. That's how our system works.

Memorandum to Judie Brown from Richard Cowden-Guido: 22 March 1988

All appeals in the Andrews case have been turned down. As such, the only possibility for freeing her according to the Florida state constitution is clemency. However, an internal cabinet rule has it that clemency is normally only granted after the prisoner is released, and that, in the Andrews case, because she is still confined, a waiver was necessary before a vote could be taken on clemency.

In addition, the state constitution does not give the Governor sole power of granting clemency, but mandates that he must have, along with his own positive vote, the support of three of six cabinet members as well. In early December 1987, before Miss Andrews' transfer out of Florida, the Florida state Parole and Probation board publicly recommended that the cabinet vote on the matter of the waiver.

Secret, however, was the administrative measure taken by the Executive Clemency Board on 9 December 1987, which was a formal alerting of the cabinet that they had until 8 March 1988, or 90 days, in which to decide whether or not to grant this preliminary step necessary to a vote on clemency itself.

Why the matter was kept secret is subject to speculation, but it was serious enough for Governor Martinez' press secretary John Peck explicitly to deny (to the press and others) on numerous occasions that any vote on clemency was imminent or even under consideration, though that was in fact the case. Mr. Peck was not the only government official to engage in explicit duplicity about the impending vote, which, given the secrecy (though not direct falsehoods as such) from the Governor and cabinet, puts the entire process under a cloud.

Not least it puts under a cloud the Governor's own vote in support of the waiver, which was joined by Attorney General Robert Butterworth and Agriculture Commissioner Doyle O'Connor. The waiver was voted down 4-3 by the deadline of 8 March 1988, with Secretary of State James Smith, Insurance Commissioner William Gunter, Education Secretary Betty Castor and Comptroller Gerald Lewis voting against the waiver.

An internal cabinet rule which can be changed at cabinet will is that a year must pass before consideration of this waiver can again be engaged. Given the strange cover-up that preceded the first vote, numerous groups, such as the American Life League, Human Life International, various Catholic bishops and so on, are calling for a suspension of this internal rule, and a public announcement of a new 90-day waiver consideration, in order to give the public a chance to make their voices heard on this case, pro and con.

[Insurance Commissioner William Gunter is the Florida Democratic Party candidate for the U.S. Senate.]

8

Instructions to the movement:

To be a serious movement, pro-life direct action must emphasize several values.

I. God is our focus. In charge of our lives. This means our lives must include:

    A: A strong prayer life: private and communal prayer; staying close to the sources of grace; Vigils, Days of Recollection.

    B: Personal sacrifices: Fasts; periods of silence; practicing obedience in our lives.

    C: Act always in charity and love, in faithfulness to God: thus we never betray one another seeking our good over theirs; love for our adversaries spells nonviolence, and though our actions and language need to be strong and truthful, we do not cross the line into the abusive.

II. A strong leader. This is vital. We may disagree with the leader, we may try to persuade him/her to adopt our position on a matter, a tactic, but nevertheless we support the leader at all times and we try to follow the lead once a decision has been reached, unless for serious personal or family reasons we cannot do so individually.

III. Acting in unity and solidarity whenever possible with the different groups in our Rescue Movement; the leadership, lawyers, rescuers, support groups. Strive never to cause dissension. Debate issues, not personalities.

IV. There are three parts to the Rescue effort: the rescue itself; and the Courtroom; and the jail sentence. All must be seen as stages of the rescue with the primary concern being the means to save lives, present and future.

> A: The Rescue. The abortion mill action is the primary rescue of those children immediately threatened.
>
> B: The Trial. The courtroom action is a secondary, but vital means to expound truth, faithfulness and love for past and present victims.
>
> C: Jail. A sentence of incarceration is offered as penance and allows much additional strategy to enhance the rescue effort and to draw others to the movement and to the truth.

Joan Andrews

To all those who have written me—from everywhere:

I wish I had the words to thank you for the love and kindness you have shown me. . . . How deeply you have touched my heart. . . . Many of you have sent me holy cards, prayer pamphlets, religious books, medals and scapulars, some have sent me packages (I could not receive these, but will see them at my sister's when I am released), others money and stamps, some have written official requests for my release, and all of you have prayed for me and given of your love. . . . I thank you with all my heart and I pray for each of you and your families daily. . . . If you were only to know how profoundly you have brought me strength and comfort. . . . [T]ruly, you allowed Our Lord to use you to bring His compassion and His Presence to me. Oh, how dear you are. And how wonderful is our God!. . .

Could I ask something more of you—something far more important than any aid you could ever give me directly or materially, but which would benefit me and yourselves, our Holy Faith, the nation, and all people beyond any ability to estimate? Would you spend some time with the little babies in your own neighborhood before they die? Maybe you'll even be able directly to save some lives, maybe not. What's even more important, you'll be there. In a sense, it may be a way to redeem the abandonment of Jesus by His apostles, when they refused to be with Him at His death—too often, we also refuse to be with Jesus for fear of the Cross, do we not?

These little ones dying today are intricately connected with the sufferings and death of Our Savior. There is a bond here that must not be overlooked. All the political action, educating, donation of funds, demonstrations, alternative work, important and necessary as these are, do not make up for an absence at the death scene. Thus, let me beg you to view your presence at the killing center in your area as the place where God wants you to be. Grab your rosary, pick up your Bible, bring your devotionals, and go out to the Calvary not far from you—where Christ is being crucified today in your midst.

Mankind abandoned the Son of God when He came to the earth to walk among us and to die for us, but remember that He never abandons any of us—not ever. So you know where He is on a Saturday morning or a Friday afternoon or a Wednesday noonday when precious infants are being killed, painfully, in your neighborhood.

Maybe you have always thought, "What can I do there?" You can pray. And you can be a presence. Our presence serves as a witness to the community of the wrongness and the evil of what goes on behind the closed doors of a killing center. Our mere presence often convinces a mother and a father not to kill their child. What is more, our presence gives solace to the bitterly wounded Heart of Jesus, and to the souls of the dying infants.

We may not be able to save their lives, but can we not plead on their behalf? And should they die, as usually happens (God forgive us!), let us lift up our hearts to God Almighty on their behalf. . . . It will be the only human love they will know on this earth. . . .

Make a commitment, I beg of you, for at least one holy hour of prayer and fasting at a death camp every week. Here I am Lord. Send me. I will go. . . .

Letter from the Winner of the 1979 Nobel Prize for Peace

Dear Joan Andrews,

This brings you my prayer and blessing that you may be only all for Jesus through Mary.

You have offered all to God and accepted all suffering for the love of Him—because you know that whatever you do to the least or for the least you do it to Jesus—because Jesus has clearly said, If you receive a little child in my name you receive Me.

We are all praying for you. Do not be afraid. All this suffering is but the kiss of Jesus—a sign that you have come so close to Jesus on the cross—so that He can kiss you.

Be not afraid—Jesus loves you—you are precious to Him—He loves you.

My prayer is always near you and for you.

God bless you.

Mother Teresa of Calcutta

Joy of the Christian

God is so very good. I feel such great peace and consolation through His gentleness and His kindness, and I know
He is touching all our pro-life people. Your deep love and
faithfulness to God's little souls gives me overwhelming comfort, so that this cell becomes a place of joy and beautiful
light! How I love all of you. How I rejoice in the consolation
and love you give to the Sacred Hearts of Jesus and Mary!

We can never get discouraged as long as we serve the
Lord. As long as we do our part, we know He will do His,
and therefore we should live in the greatest joy. Whatever
happens, we can rejoice. I don't think I have ever been hap-
pier in my life, because I feel God's presence guiding and
guarding and loving all of our people and their families, as
we offer our lives to Him, to use as He wills. What greater
joy can there be than this? None, surely.

Victory in this struggle to end the holocaust is not going
to be easy, nor painfree, but we can and must always have
great joy in our hearts and souls. And the victory to come
probably will not be soon. I am sure there will be much suffering first. But, oh, thank God we have finally realized this
and are all of us taking up the Cross we must help each other
to bear. This is a reason for great, great joy, for we are committing ourselves to God's work regardless of the cost.
Therefore, the most important step has already been taken.

The rest is in God's hands. The victory over all will
come when it comes, but at least we individually will live in
personal victory daily, in our own lives, the victory of our
wills, our hearts, our minds, our bodies, submitted to God's
will. Our souls will be freely and lovingly placed in His hands.

That's the first victory and the most important. After we
have done that we have nothing to fear from the abortionists, from the courts, from prison shackles, from the devil.
The only thing in this world to fear, truly fear, is the spirit

that dwells within ourselves over which we have control, if we have not turned that spirit over to the control of our dear God. . . . How blessed we are to have a God who will take control of us at our bidding, and who wills only our complete and total union with Him!. . . . There is nothing to be desired beyond this.

I see our people letting go more and more, growing spiritually, growing deeper in love with God, with each other, with the precious babies, and in a very real and holy way with those who engineer, permit, perpetuate and commit the holocaust. With true love for them.

I believe we have always had this love . . . but I believe our new growth is that we realize we must suffer, deeply so, and allow God to be in control, and thus I can see we are trusting Him more completely than ever before. That is why no one should feel badly for me. I am so happy. And my friends are so in love with God, I don't think it hardly entered your minds to feel sorry for me, or worry about me. I am so blessed to know each and every one of our beloved people, rescuers and supporters, all prayer warriors—gentle, loving, caring, spiritual warriors who pray with words and with actions.

I love and admire all of you so much. Please know that I am with you in prayer and in spirit. The best thing anyone can do for me is just what you have been doing: going out and protecting God's precious little children as the Lord leads you. Many times a day I sing our rescue song in my cell—Here I am, Lord. I love it so.

God bless you, and Mary keep you in her care.

Joan Andrews

[On 23 February 1988, Joan heard her first Mass since July of 1986, celebrated by fellow-rescuer Fr. John McFadden. During the first week of May 1988, there were over 1,700 rescue arrests in Operation Rescue New York, including dozens of priests, nuns, clergymen, and orthodox rabbis, as well as Bishop Austin Vaughan, and such luminaries as New York Giant tight end Mark Bavaro. Another thousand Americans were arrested during three days of Operation Rescue Philadelphia the week of July 4th. Between these two nationally organized events, over five hundred Americans were arrested in local rescues in Jackson, Mississippi; Rochester, New York; Kansas City, Kansas; Dobbs Ferry, New York; and Pittsburgh, Pennsylvania. There have thus now been more rescue arrests ion 1988 than the combined arrests from 1970 through 1987—and the specter continues to grow that the United States will no longer be able to enforce the abortion holocaust without jailing hundreds and eventually thousands of Americans first.

Meanwhile, Delaware authorities sought Joan's release from Florida officials, which the latter denied. Accordingly Joan asked to be returned to Florida, which Delaware officials granted, despite resistance from Florida. Upon her return to Broward Correctional on 17 June 1988, Joan was assaulted by a male prison guard in a violent "strip-search." An investigation is presently underway.]

For those interested

Those who wish to express an opinion on this case to Governor Robert Martinez should keep their letters short, polite, and to the point. Never more than a page: better still, three or four sentences. It could not hurt to quote Father Lisante's observation that Governor Martinez should "be open enough to recognize how unfair, how unjust is this sentence, and to pardon this woman not for any crimes she's committed but to excuse her for standing up for a moral principle. If he's a governor who knows what it is to have a conscience he'll understand what that means. . . ."

Since Governor Martinez cannot pardon Andrews on his own, but also needs the support of three other cabinet officers, copies of your letters to him should be sent to them as well. The address for all concerned is: The Capitol, Tallahassee, Florida 32399. The other cabinet officers are: Robert Butterworth, Attorney General; James Smith, Secretary of State; William Gunter, Insurance Commissioner; Doyle Conner, Commissioner of Agriculture; Betty Castor, Commissioner of Education.